Marriage and Maturity

Marriage and Maturity

The Truth About Holy Matrimony

JASON L. MOORE

RESOURCE *Publications* · Eugene, Oregon

MARRIAGE AND MATURITY
The Truth About Holy Matrimony

Resource Publications
An Imprint of Wipf and Stock Publishers
199 W. 8th Ave., Suite 3
Eugene, OR 97401

www.wipfandstock.com

PAPERBACK ISBN: 979-8-3852-4471-3
HARDCOVER ISBN: 979-8-3852-4472-0
EBOOK ISBN: 979-8-3852-4473-7

VERSION NUMBER 022025

To Karl and Sue,

who demonstrates what marriage can be
when spouses pursue maturity.

Contents

Acknowledgments

I FIRST WANT TO thank the Counselor Education faculty at Cleveland State University. They provided a foundation for me to become empowered to provide competent help to others in their greatest times of need.

I also thank Betty Barlow, my former clinical supervisor. My early days as a counselor were so much better because of her insights and mentorship.

Lastly, this book would not be a reality without all the couples I have had the privilege of working with over the years. Whether their marriages succeeded or failed, I learned a great deal from our experiences together.

Introduction

WHO COULD BRING THEMSELVES to marry a total stranger? That is precisely what happens on the Lifetime series Married at First Sight. Described as America's most controversial experiment, Married at First Sight is a reality show that lives up to its name.

How does it work? First, a panel of experts screen potential spouses for marital readiness. Afterwards, some of them are "matched" with someone with whom they are deemed to be compatible. Once each prospective participant is notified of the match, they make the decision to get married shortly after receiving the announcement. As they begin their wedding preparations, family and friends weigh in on their decision, all while being filmed by the show's production team.

On the wedding day, each soon-to-be-spouse will meet their wife or husband for the first time. The weddings are as typical as they come: family and friends, evening reception, and of course, a photographer. As the bride and groom exit the platform, they find a quiet place where they can be alone before continuing with the day's festivities. During their initial meeting, they begin the process of getting to know each other. This process will last for at least two months; afterwards, they reconvene with the experts to decide if they will continue in the marriage or get a divorce.

Sometimes, couples will renew their commitment on Decision Day, while others choose to call it quits. Not surprisingly, the criteria used to match couples is designed to ensure their compatibility for a lifetime commitment. When these marriages fail, this naturally leads to the question: if objective standards are utilized to pair people together, what could go so wrong in their relationships that they decide to part ways? Since the experts occasionally meet with the couples throughout the connecting process, and are available for 'emergency' sessions, why do some marriages still end in divorce?

Although the show is said to have a lower-than-expected success rate, one thing is clear: knowing one's spouse for only a short time prior to committing to them long-term is not the primary factor in marital terminations. If that was the case, none of the couples would survive the challenges of a video-recorded marriage to a stranger. The show also reveals that having one's privacy invaded daily, despite the inherent pressure from such an experiment, does not automatically contribute to marital dissolutions. Perhaps the show's disappointing outcomes suggest that there is some other factor underneath the challenges of marital conflicts that influences couples to either maintain or dissolve their marriages.

The Married at First Sight approach naturally leads to several questions. For instance, are these people participating in this experiment due to a sincere desire for love or a severe case of desperation? Do they really take marriage seriously? Who in their right minds would marry someone they don't know? We may never know the answers to these questions, and we don't need to. The important thing to consider is the outcome of these relationship experiments will be largely determined not by what the couples experience externally, but by who they are internally.

The premise of this book is that couples enjoy a meaningful relationship only when both parties possess the necessary maturity to approach holy matrimony with the genuine intentionality it requires. This is true not only for couples on Married at First Sight, but for couples at any stage of their marriages.

We Already Know! Really?

Why another book on marriage? Aren't there enough already in existence? Yes, there are plenty of marriage enhancement books on the market. However, there are two things that I believe sets this one apart from most others.

First, *Marriage and Maturity* focuses almost exclusively on the individual, rather than on behavior patterns. The reason for this approach is simple: external habits stem from internal realities. Most of the "how to" books on marriage concentrate on behavior modification. For example, one author described the primary reason for marital discord as a "rhythms mismatch" where partners' conflicting schedules contribute to their disconnection.[1] From my perspective, that emphasis circumvents the most important, underlying issue impacting couples today.

Another difference is that many marriage improvement resources do not challenge relationship practices that comfortably fit within modern conventional wisdom. As you can discern from the chapter headings, I do not shy away from addressing commonly embraced social norms. The truth is, none of us should; in confronting misguided relationship notions, we can arrive at properly aligned conclusions regarding the truth about holy matrimony.

Before delving into the book's content, it is worth noting that despite being marriage-centered, most of the principles and insights shared are also applicable to any serious, romantic relationship. Since many couples choose to cohabitate without the marital attachment, there are relationship realities that these couples face that are vastly similar to those experienced in monogamous marriages. As such, unmarried couples can surely benefit from the discussions in the ensuing chapters.

Contents

The focus of this book logically and necessarily considers the question, 'What is maturity'? If it is essential for marital success,[2] one

1. Fraenkel, *Sync Your Relationship, Save Your Marriage*, 3.

2. Success as applied here is not referring merely to staying together. Couples who are miserable, disconnected, and confused in their relationship may still have reasons to maintain their marriage. Here, success is measured by not only remaining with one's spouse, but having a meaningful, engaging

must understand its nature as well as how to identify it. Thus, in chapter one exploring the concept of marital maturity, along with examples of immaturity, is vital to understanding the marriage relationship as it should be.

Chapter two presents the most common reasons given for why people get married. After learning about what maturity is, the next step is to consider the basis for why marriages are so common the world over. Building off the understanding of marital maturity, this chapter will examine the sources of marital pursuits to consider if there are both proper and improper reasons for seeking a lifelong union.

After the honeymoon phase, couples begin to experience the realities of married life, even if they lived together beforehand. This new commitment, with all the attending circumstances, are now brought to the surface. Inevitably, the couple will come to realize that their differences are not always easy to resolve. In fact, for many couples, the first few years of marriage are the most challenging. The paradise experience they once relished may now be confronted with pressing marital troubles. Thus, chapter three addresses the relevance of how couples handle these potentially tumultuous times and the implications their approaches have on their growth as well as their relationships.

Even if a couple begins learning how to navigate the storms of their relationship, they sometimes recognize the need to involve someone else in it. Enter the marriage counseling session, which oftentimes entails one spouse who is eager while the other is only reluctantly participating.

For those couples who are religious, it is not uncommon for them to prefer counseling from a religious leader (i.e. pastor, rabbi, etc.). Indeed, sharing the same faith as the counselor is seen as a bonus. For the irreligious, a professional counselor, marriage and family therapist, or psychologist may be the choice. In any option, there are potential rewards and risks to the couple depending on the nature of the therapeutic process. Furthermore, the role that post-marital counseling plays in the personal development of each

relationship characterized by maturity, connectedness, and personal growth.

spouse is of no small concern. As such, various factors of this common experience will be explored in chapter four.

Whether a couple receives marriage counseling or not, some marriages will end in divorce. Not surprisingly, the divorce rate in America seems to remain steady. Numerous reasons are usually given for the persistence of divorces, with the underlying sources of the dissolution being unhappiness with the relationship. In addition, some marriages end albeit one spouse remains willing to work on improving the relationship. Thus, why marriages end that could have otherwise been salvaged, along with new perspectives on adultery, are subjects within chapter five.

The phrase "Happy Wife, Happy Life" is pervasive throughout American culture and perhaps beyond. Obviously, there is nothing wrong with a husband's desire for his wife's happiness; this is a basic relationship characteristic. However, there are various ways of understanding this phrase that will either promote or hinder marital maturity. Because of this, the notion of happiness is replaced by healthiness as the primary emphasis. What chapter six describes is an alternative to the all-too-common approach of marital fulfillment in place of something significantly better.

Merely discussing the wife's status in the marriage would be incomplete without also exploring ways of increasing one's marital maturity. Since most people who get hitched are hoping to experience marital bliss, strategies for attaining such an outcome are certainly worthy of one's attention. That is why chapter seven offers several encouraging challenges to those who desire to develop their maturity for both them and their spouses.

Chapter eight concludes with a plea to those who take marriage seriously, because not everyone does. These closing remarks are directed towards the three categories of people for whom the book was primarily written: those considering marriage, married couples in any stage of their relationships, and counselors/therapists who work with couples.

The pursuit of maturity in marriage does not have to be intimidating. Rather, welcoming the stressors of matrimony is appropriate when both parties are committed to developing the level of maturity that lifelong marital success requires. Hopefully, by the time you complete this book, you will agree.

Discussion Questions

1. If you are/were single, would you be willing to be a participant on Married at First Sight? Why or why not?

2. What has been your experience with reading marriage improvement books?

1

What is Maturity?

IN 1964, A CASE was brought before the Supreme Court involving the topic of obscenity. In that case, namely, *Jacobellis v. Ohio*, the issue was whether the conviction of a theater owner should have been upheld by the state court for showing a film that was claimed to be obscene. In Justice Potter Stewart's concurring opinion, he affirmed that the film did not satisfy the criteria for content that could be legally suppressed. Further, he argued that the film's content did not portray sexual content of a graphic nature and thus should not have been considered obscene. His famous phrase regarding questionable content, "I know it when I see it", along with careful reasoning, led to the reversal of the *Jacobellis* conviction. Consequently, a new judicial catchphrase made its way into the Court's history.

Just as Justice Stewart's phrase illustrates the challenge with defining obscenity, it is also challenging to define maturity. Indeed, we apply the notion of maturity to a variety of areas, including stocks, children, and even spirituality. Yet, applying a single definition of maturity to all these categories would not do them justice. Nevertheless, like Justice Stewart, we typically recognize maturity at work when we observe it.

For our purposes, we will focus on maturity as it relates to psychological development. That is, maturity is to be understood as an expression of mental progress and proper growth. In contrast, immaturity reflects mental stagnation or even regression. Therefore, our definition of maturity is *the outcome of proper psychological development which leads to efficient living.* This definition of maturity is applicable to marriage for several reasons.

First, most relationships will draw out of us both positive and negative emotions. As such, the handling of those emotions will be determined by the psychological capacity we have developed up to that point. For example, if a spoiled child one day does not get his way, he may throw a temper tantrum hoping to manipulate his parents into acquiescing to his desires. Why? Spoiling a child usually disrupts his capacity to manage his disappointments in appropriate ways (due to overly permissive parenting).[1] This neglect on the part of the parent often contributes to children responding to frustrations in immature ways. In contrast, a child who has developed the capacity (i.e. through proper discipline and instruction) to handle their unfulfilled desires will not throw such a tantrum. The two outcomes vary because the training and capacity are different.

Similarly, when marital strife surfaces, our responses to that strife will be based on those same two factors: training and capacity. Our minds have been trained to respond to external stimuli in either healthy or unhealthy ways. That training reinforces our present capacity, such that the result will follow. Thus, the journey towards marital maturity is via training our minds to respond to stressors with a higher capacity that ultimately contributes to lifestyle efficiency.

A second reason why this understanding of maturity applies to marriage is most people want efficiency in their relationships. What is relationship efficiency? According to dictionary.com, efficiency is defined as "performing or functioning in the best possible manner with the least waste of time and effort." Applying

1. See Direnfeld, *Marriage Rescue*, 182–3.

this definition to marriage, we can certainly see how desirable efficiency is, even if most couples seldom experience it.

In essence, nothing is more important than maturity in marriage.

Trauma & Maturity

Just as we pursue efficiency in our workplaces, our education, and our financial goals, so too we must learn to pursue efficiency in our relationships. This can only be accomplished with necessary growth which inevitably relates to maturity.

What hinders marital maturity? Normally, those who maintain an immature orientation to life and marriage can probably trace it back to childhood (or adulthood) trauma from which they have never healed. Trauma refers to those emotional wounds that cause someone to experience mental or emotional problems usually for a long time. Examples of trauma include:

- Abuse (i.e. sexual, physical, emotional)
- Neglect (i.e. parent-child relationship)
- Experiencing or witnessing domestic violence
- Diagnosis of a serious illness (mental or physical)
- Significant loss (i.e. relationship, job, health)
- Any painful past experience that leads to present-day distress

Surely, traumatic experiences directly impair our neurological development and thereby our functioning. That is, trauma corrupts the normal operations of our brains, which is why it is not uncommon for traumatized adults to exhibit childlike behavior patterns, such as:

- *Explosive tempers*
  (undisciplined anger outbursts)

- *Blatant irresponsibility*
  (unreliable with life management)
- *Lacking self-awareness*
  (inability to make emotionally intelligent connections)
- *Resistance to change/compromise*
  (opposing positive alternatives)
- *Emotional dysregulation*
  (being negatively controlled by feelings)
- *Refusing personal responsibility*
  (avoiding feelings of guilt at all costs)
- *Financial mismanagement*
  (overspending and undersaving)
- *Living a reckless lifestyle*
  (prioritizing short-term thrills over long-term planning)
- *Lacking in delayed gratification*
  (difficulty postponing immediate pleasures in consideration of future benefits)
- *Impulsivity*
  (making rash decisions with little if any forethought)
- *Taking serious matters lightly*
  (minimizing realities of genuine importance)
- *Embracing the maxim 'pleasure-before-business'*
  (prioritizing wants above needs)

Another example of emotional immaturity is what marriage researchers Julie and John Gottman refer to as stonewalling, which is the practice of ignoring someone by refusing to respond to their legitimate concerns.[2] Considering how vital communication is in marriage, remaining silent when discussions are needed can be disastrous for the relationship. Indeed, when partners fail to learn how to communicate respectfully and graciously, the likelihood

---

2. Gottman and Gottman, *10 Principles for Doing Effective Couples Therapy.*

of stonewalling increases which will only cause further damage to the marriage.

The only way for trauma to lose its impact on our lives is for our brains to get back on track with their natural processing. One way to pursue this is by talking with someone who is trained on how to provide helpful insights into your life circumstances. While professional counseling is most assuredly one way to facilitate this process, those who never avail themselves of the resources needed to heal will likely bear the burden of the trauma for years to come. In fact, this insight is consistent with one therapist's conclusion,

> Recognizing the importance of childhood trauma to the problems people have in their adult relationships was the key to unlocking the door that keeps so many people from achieving real, lasting love.[3]

In our day, we are prone to sweeping issues under the rug and moving on. Unfortunately, that same rug can be easily pulled from under us through triggers and other stressors. We should never hide from or suppress our trauma; it will show up in our lives in one way or another until we heal from it. Sadly, many people never pursue and attain the healing they need, and their spouses may suffer the consequences. This is why a noted psychiatrist explains, "Unresolved trauma can take a terrible toll on relationships."[4]

I will close this section with an illustration. Suppose your child broke his leg during a soccer game. After the doctor conducts a thorough examination of the injury, he informs your son that the future functioning of his leg is dependent on the healing he receives. Due to the desired outcome (i.e. a fully functioning leg), you and your son would likely do whatever the doctor recommended to ensure your son had a speedy and complete recovery.

Likewise, when we are afflicted with emotional or mental injuries, our capacity to function optimally (i.e. with maturity) is directly connected to our experience with healing. Therefore,

---

3. Diamond, *The Enlightened Marriage*, 49.
4. Van Der Kolk, *The Body Keeps the Score*, 213.

we too must be willing to do what is needed to facilitate our full recovery. Simply put, adequate healing from trauma is required for optimal functioning in marriage.

Maturity and Mental Health

How do we recognize maturity? Investors recognize maturity in stocks, bonds, and mutual funds once these financial gains reach a high point in their growth process. That is, we say that one's investment portfolio has matured when it increases significantly beyond where it once was. Humans are the same way. Maturity results from human development that grows beyond what it once was. We identify maturity in ourselves when we have clear evidence that we are far removed from childlike behaviors, responses, and attitudes. In contrast, immaturity reveals that we are not as far away from the average child's capacity as we should be.

Maturity is believed to be connected to positive mental health in the following ways:

- Mentally healthy people feel good about themselves.
- Mentally healthy people enjoy satisfying personal relationships.
- Mentally healthy people make their own decisions.
- Mentally healthy people are not overwhelmed by their emotions.
- Mentally healthy people have a good sense of humor.
- Mentally healthy people treat others respectfully.[5]

Commenting on number three, the author writes,

Someone who is mature and mentally healthy will not want or expect someone else to take the hard decisions

5. https://www.marriage.com/advice/marriage-fitness/what-you-need-to-know-about-marriage-and-mental-health/. (accessed on 12/9/24)

of life on their behalf, because they realize that it is their very own privilege and responsibility.[6]

Not surprisingly, a mentally healthy person is characterized by maturity; conversely, someone who is mentally unhealthy will display signs of immaturity.

These may be hard pills for some people to swallow. After all, who wants to admit that they still exhibit childlike, inefficient behaviors when in their 20's, 30's, and even beyond? Yet, this is where many people have remained, including those who bear the titles of husband and wife. If the immaturity continues, so will the consequences of it.

Consider these potential outcomes of spousal immaturity while reflecting on how unnecessary and undesirable (yet common) they are:

- Broken homes

- Traumatized children

- Financial setbacks

- Increased stress

- Violence

- Extended family disruptions

We do not want our lives to be characterized by immaturity, but many people passively and unwittingly choose it. Why? The desire for lifelong love is typically so great (especially among women) that we can easily disregard our mental health and development to pursue/welcome the chance at marriage anyway. Nevertheless, the truth remains,

> Being married—being truly married for life—requires us
> to develop a level of maturity that few other experiences
> in life can match—a maturity characterized by intense

---

6. https://www.marriage.com/advice/marriage-fitness/what-you-need-to-know-about-marriage-and-mental-health/. (accessed on 12/9/24)

vulnerability, generous amounts of forgiveness, and un-
dying patience.[7]

With so many supposed benefits that come from the marital union, it is no surprise that for many people, the reasons to
marry outweigh those to remain single. Let's explore a few of those
insights to further grasp just how relevant maturity is in such a
sacred relationship. But before that, here are a few questions for
reflection.

Discussion Questions

1. Based on the examples of maturity and immaturity, how
   would you describe your current maturity level?

2. How much healing have you experienced from any traumas
   from your past?

3. How would you describe your present mental health?

---

7. Runkel & Runkel, *The Self-Centered Marriage*, 2–3.

2

Common Reasons for Marriage

"MARRIAGE IS WORK!" LONG before I was married, I remembered hearing Sue utter those timely words. She would know, I thought. Having now been married for around 40 years, she and her husband have had their share of ups and downs. Yet, I never forgot her simple statement about marital realities and have come to realize the veracity of those three small words.

The truth is many newlyweds do not embrace this work mentality early on. Instead, they tend to focus more on delightful feelings of rapture and romance. Eventually, however, those feelings may somewhat fade, and the daily pressures of monogamous commitment emerge.

Why Marriage?

With so many marriages ending, why do so many people still prefer to tie the knot? After all, with no-fault divorces occurring regularly, what are the chances of modern marriages succeeding? Even Paul, one of the early writers of the New Testament, exclaimed, "Now to the unmarried and the widows I say: It is good for them to stay unmarried." (1 Cor. 7:8) If it was good for them to remain single, why don't we typically see it as good for us today?

In consideration of these questions, let's explore some of the common reasons people decide to assume the risk of marrying the supposed love of their lives.

One reason people still want to experience the marital relationship is out of a desire for lasting love. Clearly, one of the highest selling relationship books of all time is Gary Chapman's *The Five Love Languages*. Perhaps it is not the title that has garnered so much interest, but the subtitle: *The Secret to Love that Lasts*. This is a primary reason for pursuing what is supposed to be a lifelong commitment, namely, lasting love. In comparison, just as smiling and laughter are universal expressions of joy, so too love is a universal expression of genuine connection. For that reason, it remains at the top of the list for reasons people pursue holy matrimony.

Another reason people choose to say "I do" to their significant others is family aspirations. People are typically raised in either functional or dysfunctional family environments. For those who are reared in healthy, stable homes, they may find themselves desiring the same experience for their future family. Those who were raised in homes characterized by dysfunction may decide to pursue something better for themselves and their offspring. Whatever our backgrounds, our decisions to marry may reflect our desires which originated in our childhood experiences.

A third reason for marriage today is the fear of loneliness. Undoubtedly, we as humans have a social aspect to our personhood that seems to be lifelong. When a person seems to either minimize or repudiate having a meaningful social life, it could be a trauma response to a history of troubled relationships. Yet, connecting with others is at the heart of human relationships, and for some, that represents the essence of marriage.

Yes, a long-term relationship may prevent loneliness, but it does not provide the same privileges of a legal marriage. Also, a good marriage brings with it many benefits, along with various sources of social security. Because of these realities, many people conclude that the best way to provide stability and comfort from the loneliness trap is to get hitched for life.

Lastly, getting married is viewed as the answer to the happiness quest. Let's face it, many of us today are unhappy with our lives. As children, some of us were psychologically maimed due to living in drama-filled households and communities. During our high school years, we might have been bullied, teased, and academically unfulfilled. Upon entering adulthood, we struggled with having meaningful relationships while lacking career ambitions. Surely, there must be some way to experience happiness in this stressful world! For many of us, the solution to our quest for happiness is to marry someone who will meet our needs in ways that nothing or no one else did.

On the surface, there is nothing wrong with desiring marriage for the aforementioned reasons. Indeed, they are all believed to come with the full package of a lifelong commitment to one's spouse. On deeper reflection however, there is a problem with getting married with these goals as the primary factors in the decision. The concern with marrying someone merely for the reasons mentioned above is that they collectively disregard relevant, guaranteed aspects of the marital journey.

Other Perspectives

When was the last time you heard someone say they wanted to get married for one or more of the following reasons: the hopes of pursuing more personal growth, reaching higher levels of maturity, or being challenged to become better versions of themselves? Have you ever heard these statements included in the traditional examples of wedding vows? Probably not, even though "Few things in life ask us to grow up as much as our marriage, and few things can."[1]

Despite the unavoidable reality of the ways in which marriage stretches us, most people do not consider that factor as front and center in their relationships. How do we know? Just reflect on the reactions that many spouses display when marital conflicts begin.

---

1. Runkel and Runkel, *Screamfree Marriage*, 64.

Rather than embracing them as functional, normal, and educational aspects of the relationship, some spouses may become disillusioned at these distressing experiences. Some may find themselves thinking that they did not sign up for a marriage involving (sometimes intense) repeated conflicts. What these contemplations reveal is that the discouraged spouse was not actually prepared for the emotional realities that come along with tying the knot.

To be clear, merely desiring marriage does not mean one possesses the maturity for one.

Conflicts are not desirable for any relationship, just as straining and grunting while strength training are not desirable for athletes and bodybuilders. But the same motto that applies in the gym usually applies in marriage: no pain, no gain. Obviously, pain in the marital sense is not physical, but can be emotional and psychological. The difficulty of struggling through stressful conversations and circumstances can seem overwhelming at times, but these challenges come with the territory. Thankfully, they can yield delightful rewards for the couples that develop the maturity to push through them.

If the couple does not develop such needed skills, they may not only hurt themselves emotionally, but also physically. As Tara Pope-Parker states,

> Conflict is an inevitable part of marriage, and many couples can fight without its taking a toll on their health. But certain styles of argument can result in high levels of stress and are associated with serious health problems.[2]

In the best-case scenario, couples will begin the marriage with this understanding rather than being surprised by disheartening times down the road.

---

2. Parker-Pope, *For Better*, 114.

Now What?

If you are considering marriage at this phase of your life, I hope you will not become discouraged from your interest. If you are already married, I trust you will be further enlightened by the topics covered. If you are a counseling professional who works with couples, my hope is that these insights will be influential in your therapeutic sessions. Whatever your status, I trust you will discover new ideas that can be implemented into your life and/or your practice.

For now, let me leave you with this thought: our reasons for our pursuits will be directly connected to our reactions in either acquiring or missing out on the desired outcome. If we merely pursue marriage for emotional yet naive reasons, we may be in for rude awakenings. If the maturity needed to cope with such awakenings is lacking, matters will indeed be made worse.

However, if we pursue marriage with a willingness to embrace any unknown complications, we can prepare our hearts and minds with commitment, unconditional love, and above all, maturity to face them resolutely. As noted author Carol Dweck writes,

> A no-effort relationship is a doomed relationship, not a great relationship. It takes work to communicate accurately and it takes work to expose and resolve conflicting hopes and beliefs.[3]

The way we begin marriage has implications for the path ahead, be it growth and understanding, or heartache and misery. How will you handle the trouble that threatens the paradise you envisioned? Hopefully not like the couple you will read about in the next chapter.

Discussion Questions

1. If you are hoping to get married one day, what are the reasons for your desire?

3. Dweck, *Mindset*, 152.

2. If you are married, why did you get married?

3. Should marriage require work, or should it be relatively easy? Why?

3

Trouble in Paradise

IN DECEMBER OF 2021, it was announced that Rep. Madison Cawthorn (R-NC) and his wife were divorcing after only eight months
of marriage. According to several internet sources, Cawthorn and
his wife encountered several challenges associated with his new
position in Congress.[1] In one statement, he suggested that the
couple was originally committed to their marriage. However, the
struggles and strains of being elected to Congress, leading to a lack
of balance in the relationship, led to its demise. The ultimate reason given for the separation was "irreconcilable differences."

Ironically, wedding pictures of the representative and his wife
portray them as one of the happiest couples you could imagine. In
one photo, the couple stood in front of a huge cross that had been
adorned with a colorful flower assortment. Yet, only eight months
later, they have differences that are said to be irreconcilable. What
happened? I reserve specific discussion points on divorce for a
later chapter. Here, the emphasis is on the unwillingness to address
the troubles within marriage with the necessary maturity that such
a sacred union demands.

---

1. https://nypost.com/2021/12/23/rep-madison-cawthorn-announces-
divorce-eight-months-into-marriage/ (accessed on 12/12/24)

Is It Really a Big Deal?

This outcome is tragic for several reasons. First, Rep. Cawthorn is a conservative Republican, which usually signifies a strong commitment to traditional family values (i.e. honoring one's marital vows). One would think that a public figure embracing conservative politics would be more committed to his personal family relationships. This is not to say that Republicans tend to emphasize traditional family values more so than others. However, appealing to the stress his political life put on his marriage is paradoxical considering that family is supposed to come before one's career. Be that as it may, such a young and rising star in Congress, along with his then-wife, could have set a better example for both his Party, their families, and their country.

Another reason this eight-month marriage is a relationship travesty is that it undermines the nature of marital devotion. While lip service was given to the notion of commitment, the proof is in the pudding. No one who divorces after such a short time understands marital responsibilities, much less marital maturity. Indeed, how can either of them claim to have truly loved each other if such a short stint in oneness eroded over external circumstances?

It may be trite, but it is true: love is commitment to someone and their well-being, not mere feelings of romance. For this couple, they seemed to have confused the two and perhaps tied the knot for superficial reasons.

Rep. Cawthorn and his ex-wife are certainly not alone in their short-lived marriage; neither are they alone in their decision to allow social problems and stressors to tear them apart. Yet, these realities are not to be celebrated, but rather represent the throwaway mentality of many within our contemporary society. This approach essentially means that if something is not working well for you, discard it and find something better. Sadly, those who get married with this mindset may eventually apply it to what is supposed to be their most important relationship.

Premarital Trouble

Even before one's marriage begins, trouble may be looming on the horizon. For instance, I recently heard about a man who agreed to marry the mother of his children, but only if she first lost weight. From my understanding, they have several children together, and during their relationship (including multiple pregnancies), the mom put on more pounds than he is happy with. On the surface, his ultimatum seems cruel, unloving, and lacking in empathy. Also, she seems to be hurting because of not being accepted as she is. I can imagine her thinking, "If he was willing to have children with me, he should be willing to marry me." However, with further considerations, his approach might become more understandable.

First, she is aware of her size, whatever it is, so she does not have to be alarmed or offended by his stance. Disappointed perhaps, but not offended. Technically, he has the right to withhold himself from her as she did not require marriage prior to having children together. In this sense, he might have hurt her feelings, but he has committed no wrong in his pre-marital rejection of her. As one reflective wife acknowledges, "many [men] want to be married to a woman who keeps improving herself."[2]

Further, the question must be asked, "Is she resistant to losing weight, or just not making progress fast enough?" If the former, why would she resist making positive changes that could enhance both her life and the lives of her children (and possible husband)? Surely, we should accept things in others that they cannot change; are we not justified in challenging them to change things they can?

Moreover, if the latter is the reason, grace and understanding could factor into his future considerations with her. If she is attempting to lose weight, there is a clear basis for patience and compassion, even support. If her actions reveal effort and not resistance, she needs encouragement, not rejection. Overall, if maturity is at work in both parties, he will adjust his approach accordingly, while she will make a deliberate effort to better herself by losing weight and thereby becoming a healthier version of herself.

2. Endrei and Endrei, *Glue*, 75.

When spouses do not consistently strive for self-improvement, they can inadvertently contribute to their spouses' temptation towards someone else, be it emotional or sexual. Indeed, personal progress is reasonably more attractive and appealing than laziness. As Patti Endrei, whose comments are addressed to wives, but could also be applied to husbands, explains,

> One of the best lines of defense against the potential 'other woman' is to keep your husband focused on you by periodically and purposefully improving yourself.[3]

In what has been deemed the most extensive survey of romantic relationships ever produced, researchers gathered data from around 100,000 couples throughout the world. When discussing their findings regarding the topic of love in relationships, the authors made these observations,

> Many people have the notion that a committed relationship gives them a free pass to stop worrying about their looks; but that can be a risky assumption . . . This is *not* a good normal or a healthy relationship dynamic . . . When men or women are sexually dissatisfied or unhappy with a partner's appearance, it has an adverse impact on the couple's intimacy.[4]

These are even more reasons demonstrating why marital maturity is crucial for marital contentment and stability.

Rethinking Anger

In addition to the necessity of mindfulness regarding one's appearance, reflecting on one's approach to anger is also required. Normally, when a person erupts with anger outbursts, or presents with even mild, ongoing agitation, we associate it with immediate circumstances. In other words, we think that she is angry because the store was all out of an item she needed. Or he is angry because

---

3. Endrei and Endrei, *Glue*, 75.
4. Northrup et al, *The Normal Bar*, 124, 128.

the congested traffic made him late to work. No doubt, anger can be merely circumstantial, but sometimes it is much deeper than that.

Consider this analogy; while walking down the street, you mistakenly bump into someone's arm containing a tiny scratch. He may not respond at all; if he does, the response will likely reflect only mild discomfort. Now, imagine walking down another street and accidently bumping into someone else's arm containing a third-degree burn. His reaction is likely going to be much stronger. Why? The deeper the wound, the stronger the reaction. This reality also applies to emotional wounds.

Many people who get married have suppressed their wounds, only to have them emerge when their well-meaning spouses "bump into" them in some way. When this happens, the wounded spouse may lash out, making the situation worse than what it would have been had the proper healing taken place. Not knowing how to respond, the other spouse then chooses to match that negative energy, resulting in an explosive argument. How could this scenario have been prevented?

First, the spouse with the deep-seated wounds could have pursued the necessary healing so that he could function more optimally in the marriage. In addition, the other spouse could have learned how to better manage her own emotions to avoid being unfairly drawn into her husband's unresolved trauma reaction. After all, matching your spouse's negative energy is not the noble response; transcending it is.

The Famous Iceberg

Many therapists are aware of the Anger Iceberg, which graphically lists a variety of emotions (i.e. hurt, disappointment, stress, guilt, frustration, grief, etc.) underneath the surface of the presenting emotion (i.e. anger). Whenever clients display a pattern of anger, a counselor may discuss the iceberg with them to ascertain the exact source of the indignation. This process facilitates engagement with the root causes of this potentially destructive emotion and thereby directs the process towards anger management and emotional regulation.

Whenever a spouse exhibits self-sabotaging anger, it may not be directly related to the marriage; it could be the result of unattended emotions or unresolved trauma that the person has never explored. For example, if spouses never heal from their histories of severe life tragedies and disappointments, they may be more prone to anger outbursts than spouses who are content with the trajectory of their lives. If a spouse has never recovered from feelings of guilt and shame over past indiscretions, he may be more likely to lash out at others than a spouse who has found peace with the outcomes of his choices.

The point is, sometimes anger is more about the past than the present. The good news is anyone can experience healing in the present regardless of what they experienced in the past. When healing does not occur, more and more trouble in paradise is essentially inevitable.

Living with an angry, argumentative spouse can be draining, as is described in the following proverbs:

> Better to live on a corner of the roof than share a house with a quarrelsome wife [or husband]. (Prov. 21:9)

> Better to dwell in the wilderness, than with a contentious and angry woman [or man]. (Prov. 21:19)

Nevertheless, it does not have to lead to marital erosion. Once a spouse develops the self-awareness to consider the true source of his/her anger, the healing process can begin. Indeed, paradise lost can become paradise restored if the couple works together to uncover the meaning behind one's anger. Only then can the anger symptoms subside, and a growing relationship emerge.

What About Children?

What would our society be like if parents approached their relationships with their children similar to how many spouses approach their marriages? Imagine the overwhelmed parent one day telling their child, "We are not compatible" or "We have irreconcilable differences." As a result, the parent decides to place the child in foster care. People would be outraged at the blatant immaturity and scandalous behavior of parents who would rather separate from their child than work with them through the difficulties of life. Why is there no such outrage when spouses do this to one another?

Calvin Roberson, a marriage counselor and one of the experts on the hit series Married at First Sight, echoes this sentiment with a no-nonsense approach,

> Most of us would never consider leaving our children as a solution to the problems they present. . .The same tenacity should exist between the people who brought the children into the world . . . divorce . . . is a coward's way out.[5]

Yes, a child is different, and there may even be occasions where a parent decides to banish their child from the home due to an ongoing pattern of behavioral infractions. However, the purpose for the removal is usually corrective and is temporary, not punitive and permanent. In either case, the principle is the same. Those who are unwilling to abandon their children due to their familial connection should be equally unwilling to abandon their spouses for the same reason.

From Bad to Worse

The fallout that oftentimes results from the presence of one or two immature marital partners can be catastrophic to individuals, families, as well as the broader society. A recent example illustrates just how serious neglecting marital maturity can be. In December of 2024, a 15-year-old girl entered her small Christian school and opened fire inside her classroom. Natalie "Samantha" Rupnow killed two people and wounded six others, two of whom were in critical condition shortly thereafter.

5. Roberson, *Marriage Ain't for Punks*, 14–15.

Without knowing the specific motive for the shooting, court reports revealed that Natalie's parents married and divorced a total of three times. During their separations, she was transported between their homes multiple times during the week.[6] In addition, Natalie was reportedly meeting with a counselor due to the traumatizing family life she was subjected to. Furthermore, news reports mentioned that her father once posted a picture on social media of the two of them at a shooting range as he taught his young daughter how to shoot a rifle. What was he thinking?

Much more could be said about this devastating tragedy, but this much we know; Natalie's parents evidently devalued their own pursuit of marital maturity. Now, we see the horrible damage that their negligence has contributed to. While ultimate blame for Natalie's heinous actions lies at her own feet, her chronically unstable home environment appears to have been a strong contributing factor to the crimes she committed.

Trouble Doesn't Last Always

In reference to the couple I mentioned in the beginning of this chapter, here is a point to ponder. The primary reason for most divorces is not irreconcilable differences or incompatibility, it is immaturity. Many people have not acquired the awareness or mental development needed to grasp the complexities of the life-long commitment they supposedly want. More importantly, many people do not prioritize their own growth and maturity even after they become someone's spouse. Unfortunately, it is only after they have entered into holy matrimony that this realization becomes evident.

If spouses developed the capacity to see their difficulties as opportunities rather than threats, they could more naturally triumph over them. This is a principle that works in virtually every area of life, not just marriage. Think about it; if a student sees a failing grade as a mandate to increase her study time, that will be

6. https://www.washingtonpost.com/nation/2024/12/17/madison-wisconsin-school-shooter-natalie-rupnow/ (accessed on 12/18/24)

more helpful than viewing it as a reflection of her intellectual deficiencies. If an employee views the reprimand from his supervisor as a challenge to do better, he will become more productive than he would if he felt attacked, belittled, and unappreciated following the meeting. How we interpret our interactions and encounters with others impacts how we respond to them.

In marriage, if we interpret the stressful moments as negative, meaningless engagements, we will get nowhere. If we can learn to reframe our conflicts into more healthy opportunities for improvement, brighter days will be ahead.

Character is forged more often in the unpleasantries of life than in the pleasant moments. To truly become better versions of ourselves, we must commit to facing any disputes and disagreements with the right attitude, a healthy perspective, and of course, a reasonable amount of maturity. If we do, the trouble in paradise may come to be viewed as not so troubling after all. In fact, momentary difficulties could be blessings in disguise. As two marriage researchers concluded,

> Research indicates that 86% of unhappily married couples that stay together and work on their marriage report being much happier later on in life.[7]

Every couple has the capacity to make conflicts work for them rather than against them. Practice it, and chances are, you will not be disappointed. If you feel like you have tried and seemingly failed, it may be time to consult a neutral, unbiased third party. But be careful; not everyone who provides marriage counseling is adequately trained for it.

Discussion Questions

1. Have you ever ended a relationship after only a short time? If so, explain.

---

7. Fillmore and Barnhart, *Happily Ever After*, 17.

2. Is it cruel to refuse to marry someone due to some unpleasant physical characteristic?

3. How do you express anger, and what helps you manage it?

4. To what extent should parents be held responsible for the crimes their minor children commit?

4

Selective Marital Counseling

IN MY ROLE AS a counselor, I have seen the good, the bad, and the ugly in working with couples. There have been moments of great distress, as well as moments of celebration. Ultimately, it was not I who made the difference; instead, it was the couple deciding the future of their relationship. Yet, I did not always view it like this.

When I first started working with couples, I naively believed that whether their marriages failed or succeeded was dependent on my capacity to help them. If they decided not to return and then proceed with a divorce, it was because I did not take the correct approach. If they continued in counseling and made significant progress, perhaps I chose the correct theoretical orientation and applied all the right microskills that I learned as a student. While the counselor can and does impact the session, the ultimate outcome thereof is not entirely dependent on the therapist. For those of us working with couples, we know that this is a huge relief.

Often seen as a last resort, marriage counseling is sometimes viewed with a negative connotation. For many people, counseling is only for couples who are experiencing extremely difficult circumstances that they have not been able to resolve alone. Thus, they locate a therapist who might be able to help them navigate the rough terrain that now characterizes their relationship. Certainly, this scenario is typical within the scope of marriage counseling. However, it could also be viewed from a different perspective.

The Role of the Counselor

Counseling is designed to help people by providing them with objective, unbiased insights through an introspective process. In other words, the counselor gently guides the sessions so that clients can discover the solutions to their problems themselves. Rather than giving advice, the counselor facilitates reflective interactions with the client to promote self-discovery and personal responsibility. What this really means is that marriage counseling is designed to help couples help themselves. Here is the way one insightful counselor explained his approach,

> When I meet couples for the first time I tell them that I absolutely will listen to their complaints about each other. However, while doing so, I'm really interested in figuring out each person's contribution to distress.[1]

Why does he reveal his therapeutic style up front? "If partners don't take responsibility for their contributions to the distress, no matter how big or small, things won't improve."[2]

That said, there are certain caveats that come along with the counseling experience.

Premarital Counseling

First, engaged couples can avail themselves of therapeutic options prior to their wedding days. However, they may want to avoid putting too much stock in premarital counseling programs. Albeit premarital counseling can help couples explore topics that had not been previously considered, it is inadequate to prepare them for the complexities of the challenges that lie ahead. Indeed, past

1. Direnfeld, *Marriage Rescue*, 1.
2. Direnfeld, *Marriage Rescue*, 1.

and present reflections alone are insufficient to secure desirable outcomes in the future.

The point here is not to avoid premarital counseling; as one who is certified in it (i.e. SYMBIS), I know it can be a good thing. Rather, a couple can alleviate future marital disappointments and disillusionment if they keep expectations of the premarital counseling experience low while maintaining high expectations for their own growth.

In some cases, premarital counseling may provide indicators that a couple may want to rethink getting married. If the couple is both open and honest about what they discuss, insights gleaned from these sessions may be very eye-opening. Whatever the outcome, couples should not end their historical and personality explorations with premarital counseling; keep learning about your relationship!

Religious Counseling

A second caveat about marital counseling pertains to the selection of the therapist. Many people have participated in what is known as pastoral counseling. This form of counseling utilizes a religious specialist (i.e. pastor, priest, rabbi, etc.) rather than a licensed professional. For those in these religious communities, the reasons for this choice are obvious.

First, meeting with an unlicensed, religious leader is free. Certainly, the financial incentive may be at the top of the list for their selection. Secondly, there is a certain level of trust that many people place in their spiritual leaders. Generally, those in positions of spiritual leadership usually have the best of motives and sound reputations. For counselee candidates, this is enough to utilize pastoral services.

A third reason for pursuing pastoral counseling is the religious professional may have experience working with other couples. When one works in a sizable community, it is likely that at some point the spiritual shepherd will have the experience of counseling couples in distress. Thus, other candidates for counseling may take notice of this and consider that a reason to visit the cleric's office.

Lastly, many religious couples would prefer to meet with someone who shares their same values and perspectives. Thus, meeting with a pastoral counselor who can reference their sacred Scriptures during the session has special appeal. For these reasons, religious practitioners may be inclined to take advantage of pastoral help when their relationships are in trouble.

Concerns with Religious Counseling

The reasons for pursuing pastoral counseling are certainly understandable. Indeed, pastoral counselors can learn many of the same interventions and strategies that professional counselors use. However, it must be emphasized that religious leaders are no more qualified to be counselors than counselors are qualified to be religious leaders. Undoubtedly, the two professions are vastly different. Unfortunately, selecting religious counselors who are not properly trained in counseling skills, theories, and practices can have an adverse impact on your marriage. This is demonstrably true for the following reasons.

First, if you are personally affiliated with the pastoral counselor, there is always the possibility that the spiritual leader will lack neutrality and objectivity. It is no secret that in religious communities, friendships develop between the leader and the congregants. When this happens, judgment may be clouded, especially when deep-seated connections have been established.

For example, suppose Bobby and Lisa are having major difficulties in their marriage. They decide to contact Pastor Jones for marriage counseling. Lisa has been a member of Pastor Jones's church for many years, while Bobby has only been there since his recent marriage to Lisa. Pastor Jones is much more acquainted with Lisa and knows more about her than Bobby. As a result, there is a prolonged friendship that has been established between the pastor and Lisa.

This reality may become a problem during their counseling sessions. For instance, if Lisa expresses heartfelt sadness during their meetings, the pastor may become more inclined towards compassion and sympathy for her. In addition, depending on the closeness of their friendship, Pastor Jones may view Lisa as family, while not necessarily regarding Bobby in that manner. In this situation, it may not be long before the subjective bias surfaces, as personal feelings towards Lisa may become more obvious with the pastor's approach.

Professional counselors are forbidden from counseling friends and family members if objectivity is not possible.[3] However, this standard does not apply to pastoral counselors who decide for themselves who they will and will not meet with.[4] As such, regarding our example, there is the real possibility that Pastor Jones may not help the couple, but only Lisa. This is the sad reality of some pastoral counseling sessions. Where clear objectivity and neutrality cannot be established, the pastoral counselor would do well to refer the couple to someone who has such capabilities.

Where is the Evidence?

A second concern with pastoral counseling is that the approach may not be centered on evidence-based practices. In any mental health profession, practitioners seek to utilize approaches with clients that have a history of being effective in producing positive changes. Researchers invest time, money, and effort to discover such practices to make them available to other licensed professionals. If evidence-based practices were not available, the counselor would resort to whatever methods he/she deemed proper at that moment. In that case, the result may be ineffective counseling that could be counterproductive.

3. American Counseling Association, *Code of Ethics*, A.5.d.

4. There are voluntary licensing and certification programs for pastoral counselors. However, in most cases, religious leaders are not required to attain such credentials prior to conducting counseling sessions with members of their congregations.

A Modern Example

One day while channel surfing, I stumbled upon a televised church service led by one of the most well-known Christian leaders of the 21st century. During his sermon, he discussed a recent encounter he had with a despondent parishioner. The man shared with the pastor that he had been feeling sad and depressed and thus came to him for help. What was the pastor's response? He encouraged the gentleman to go home and watch a few funny movies and that should take care of his problem. Supposedly, the pastor was right! He explained that the man later acknowledged how helpful the pastor's suggestion was. So, does this imply that watching humorous films can alleviate the symptoms of depression?

There are several observations about this experience that are worth noting. First, it is likely that the man who went to the pastor for help was facing very mild symptoms. The reason is that a more severe form of depression (i.e. major depressive disorder) would have likely been unaffected by an attempt to pursue experiences involving laughter. In fact, the man might have even lacked the motivation to approach the pastor in the first place, let alone implement his suggestion. That said, assuming that the pastor's recommendation was truly helpful, it still sounded like a spur-of-the-moment consideration rather than a thoughtful and reflective approach that has been known to help others with the same problem.

Another issue with the pastor's response is that it promotes the quick-fix mentality in dealing with mental health challenges. Simply viewing humorous content, even if therapeutic, may not be enough, especially for treating depressive symptoms or someone who is grieving loss. More reliable approaches have been studied and verified as helpful mechanisms for moving people past feelings of sadness. Incidentally, the pastor's idea, though unconventional, is not the problem; the underlying approach is. In a genuine counseling relationship, a treatment plan would be developed, in consultation with the client, that could (in theory) entail the inclusion of positive material (i.e. comedies). However, that would only be one aspect of the plan, as that task alone would be deemed in-sufficient for seeking long-lasting, positive changes with the client.

The counseling experience must be taken seriously when people are facing the most distressing moments of their lives. If the pastoral counselor is unaware of evidence-based practices for marital therapy, he should not be counseling couples. Indeed, he runs the risk of causing further harm to the couple's relationship. Therefore, any pastoral counselor who endeavors to help couples facing marital problems should avail himself of the research per-taining to evidence-based practices relevant to effective couples therapy.[5]

Being Held Accountable

The third reason why pastoral counseling may not be best for to-day's couples is the lack of accountability on the part of the religious leader. In becoming a professional counselor, one must spend hun-dreds of hours working directly with clients during the practicum and year-long internship.[6] During this time, the counselor-trainee is supervised by a licensed clinical counselor who has a supervisor designation. Even after the counselor becomes licensed, the super-vision continues.[7] The purpose of the supervision is for the more experienced counselor to provide honest feedback to the counsel-ing student/new counselor about her practices, paperwork, and overall counseling approaches. In contrast, pastoral counselors may never have anyone to which they are accountable for their counseling sessions. In the field of counseling, more accountability is better than less.

---

5. See Gottman and Gottman, *10 Principles*.

6. The requirements are similar for those planning to become Licensed Marriage and Family Therapists.

7. Licensed counselors are only required to have supervision until they are independently licensed. This is usually several years after their initial licensure. Yet, continuing education is required for licensure maintenance so that coun-selors stay up-to-date on current research and developments within the field.

To illustrate, if a counseling student says or does something improper during a session, it can be discussed and corrected when he meets with his supervisor. However, if Pastor Jones did or said something that was not in keeping with proper counseling techniques, no one may ever know about it. Not only that, but there is also no one there to provide him with any feedback on his approach. This could result in greater harm to the couple as well as less self-awareness and growth for the pastor. Both results could be avoided with proper supervision and feedback.

Why is accountability so important in counseling? People who come to counseling are seeking guidance and direction for getting through one of the lowest points in their lives. In their seeming desperation, they are relying on the counselor to help them through this most difficult life experience. Because of the possibility of further damage occurring in the context of the counseling sessions, licensed counselors (or their agencies) will typically carry liability insurance to protect themselves from both false accusations and even lawsuits.

Counseling is serious business.

Where is the accountability for the average pastoral counselor? There is none. Consider this scenario: Let's suppose a woman is meeting with her pastor to decide whether she should reveal a potentially damaging secret to her husband. After sharing explicit details about the issue, the pastor 'counsels' her to dignify her husband by sharing the truth. She heeds his recommendation and later that day discloses the matter to her husband. In a fit of rage, the husband lashes out and attacks her, resulting in her death.

Due to the power dynamic of the counselor-client relationship, the pastoral counselor bears some responsibility for this tragedy. For, the woman both trusted and responded to the advice from her pastor. Yet, despite his direct contribution to that fatal attack, he would likely never be held accountable for his counseling incompetence.

This situation is not meant to suggest that it would be better for a wife to maintain a posture of secrecy from her husband. Rather, the point is that it is not the counselor's responsibility to inform clients about what they should do. Instead, the counselor is to help the clients discover for themselves what is in their best interest without resorting to well-meaning antidotes or recommendations. Indeed, the pastor who merely gives marital advice is not engaging in proper counseling practices, period.

Remember, counseling others is not to be taken lightly.

What is Needed?

Objectivity, evidence-based practices, education, and feedback/supervision are all designed to lead to one thing: counseling competence. It is virtually impossible to reach a level of competence in marital therapy without them. However, this does not mean that religious leaders like Pastor Jones are unable to help any couple that would meet with him. To the contrary, it means that they need similar training to that received by mental health professionals. If they are not willing to pursue such training, the best course would be referring couples to someone who is properly credentialed and who takes counseling more seriously.

Lacking the education and training for competence development can lead to inefficient outcomes in couples therapy. But why take the chance? As I stated, those who position themselves to provide counseling services to others must be committed to learning more about both mental health realities as well as marital counseling strategies. They must educate themselves on techniques and orientations that have a demonstrated track record of providing needed help to couples. Without a commitment to counseling education, competence in helping couples will likely never be established.

I understand that pastoral counselors simply desire to help those who come to them for assistance. Indeed, I have no doubt that these spiritual leaders mean well, and I imagine that some people have benefited from their input. However, good motives do not always lead to good judgment. In fact, one of the reasons I decided to become a counselor was due to the ineffective pastoral counseling I once received during one of the lowest points in my life. After those experiences, I realized I wanted to become the kind of counselor I wish I had during those challenging times. Thus, for me, this topic is not merely theoretical, it is personal.

Back to Maturity

What does all of this have to do with marital maturity? For struggling couples who are looking for help with their relationships, don't take the easy way out. Find someone who is a licensed professional and has experience working with couples. There are various ways to find someone who is qualified to assist you. Remember, there is nothing wrong with getting a neutral third-party's insights on your relationship; in fact, it can be a good thing. Take the step if needed and be prepared to be challenged. If you are still leaning towards pastoral counseling, remember this; you get what you pay for. If you want the best kind of intervention, work with someone who is best prepared to provide it.

What if counseling is pursued, but it still does not help? This is always a possibility; couples who participate in marriage counseling cannot receive a 'satisfaction guaranteed' promise from the counselor. Counseling is only effective if both spouses are committed to working through their issues in constructive ways. Unfortunately, counseling sessions sometimes reveal that one or both parties is unwilling to work on the relationship. Perhaps their only reason for engaging in therapy was to present themselves as being outwardly interested when truthfully, they were inwardly apathetic.

Marriages that do not progress during or after counseling may become worse, leading to the ultimate decision to separate. But why? In some ways, the spouse that is on the receiving end of the separation is more like the spouse who initiates it. How can that reality be rationalized? Maybe it can't, as we will see in the next chapter.

Discussion Questions

1. If you are married, did you receive premarital counseling? Why or why not?

2. If you are religious and interested in counseling, would you prefer meeting with someone of the same faith? Why?

3. Have you ever considered counseling but decided against it? Explain.

5

The Hypocrisy of Divorce

IF A PERSON BELIEVES one thing, but their actions are inconsistent with their beliefs, they may suffer mental distress as a result. If so, they may be displaying a condition known as cognitive dissonance. This technical phrase is based on the reality that people tend to be true to themselves in most situations. In other words, our actions typically follow our core beliefs about ourselves and the world. When our actions do not align with our values, distress may result.

For our purposes, we will replace our understanding of cognitive dissonance with a similar yet potentially offensive term: hypocrisy. Although this word is most directed towards religious people, as we will see, religion is not the only sphere of human experience where hypocrisy can be readily detected.

Vows Revisited

A quick internet search for traditional marriage vows will likely yield some version of the following:

> I, _____, take thee, _____, to be my lawfully wedded wife (husband), to have and to hold from this day forward, for

better, for worse, for richer, for poorer, in sickness and in health, to love and to cherish, till death do us part.

On the wedding day, these sentiments are usually recited glibly and excitedly. Yet, we know that in many cases, these sacred utterances are eventually disregarded for spurious reasons. But why?

Let's face it, there is an inherent difficulty in honoring vows that we don't always want to honor. In any marriage, there will be moments of frustration, tension, anger, and even resentment towards one's spouse. In these situations, our natural inclination may not always be to reflect on that glorious wedding day when we made promises before God and others. However, considering today's replacement mentality regarding marriage, perhaps it is time for deeper reflections on the nature and relevance of these special promises.

Beginning with the phrase "from this day forward", this statement naturally suggests longevity. That is, vowing to be wed to your partner "from this day forward" is the foundation for commitment. Nevertheless, we know that for many, these words are easier to recite than to live out. Why? Perhaps the next phrase sheds light on the answer. "For better, for worse" is like teaching someone about forgiveness. And as C. S. Lewis once said, "Everyone thinks forgiveness is a lovely idea until he has something to forgive."[1]

Similarly, most people affirm the value of remaining with one's spouse through the "worse" situations until they are confronted with the realities of what such a commitment entails. Honoring this aspect of one's wedding vows involves the willingness to endure such experiences as poverty ("for poorer") and illness ("in sickness"). For many couples, these are not deal-breaking problems. After all, wealth is only amassed by a select few, and illness will likely come to everyone at some point. The deeper challenge comes from both genuinely embracing and weathering the challenges of marriage "till death."

1. Lewis, *Mere Christianity*, 115.

When we consider the ongoing divorce rates in America, one wonders if many spouses truly plan to spend the rest of their lives together. In fact, according to the U.S. National Center for Health Statistics, in 2022, there were over 600,000 divorces in America.[2] Despite the high number of marital separations, there are many available resources across the nation that are geared towards helping couples stay together. Nevertheless, for many spouses, such resources are disregarded, minimized, or neglected. This is where our discussion on hypocrisy is brought to focus.

What is Hypocrisy?

In the denotative sense, a hypocrite is essentially an actor. That is, hypocrites play roles in public that they do not actually embrace in private. Normally, we associate hypocrisy with religious people who do not practice what they preach. However, hypocrisy can be seen even among secular people with no religious affiliation. For our purposes, hypocrisy in marriages today exists when one spouse separates from the other on nebulous grounds, despite the other spouse's interest in sustaining the marriage.[3]

In his book *When Sinners Say "I Do"*, Dave Harvey writes,

> Marriage is the union of two people who arrive toting the luggage of life. And that luggage always contains sin.[4]

Harvey highlights a crucial reality regarding holy matrimony. Despite how glorious both the bride and groom may appear on their wedding day, there are unseen dynamics from their past (and perhaps present) that will inevitably impact their relationship. Subconsciously, spouses recognize this truth without knowingly giving it much attention. Unless there are serious, overt

---

2. https://www.cdc.gov/nchs/fastats/marriage-divorce.htm (accessed on 1/13/24).

3. There are certainly more serious matters that come up in marriage, such as ongoing adultery or domestic violence. However, those cases represent the exceptions rather than the norm.

4. Harvey, *When Sinners Say "I Do"*, 15.

circumstances that command immediate attention, the "luggage of life" seems to be swept under the rug until one spouse later uses it as a reason to justify terminating the marriage. That is marital hypocrisy.

The connotative understanding of hypocrisy lies in one's inability to apply the same standards to oneself that are applied to others. In other words, hypocrisy in this sense represents one's failure to live up to one's own expected ideals. Interestingly enough, a biblical warning against hypocrisy is found in the admonition to avoid thinking more highly of ourselves than we ought to (Rom. 12:3). In addition, Jesus is recorded as using his harshest tone in condemning the hypocrisy of those regarded as religious leaders (Matt. 23).

Every spouse, regardless of their accomplishments, qualities, or social prominence, is flawed; deeply flawed. Surely, a quality marriage will not be realized by those who are full of pride, but only those who are full of humility. A humble person not only acknowledges their own shortcomings, but is ready, willing, and able to extend grace and understanding to those of their spouse. Without grace and empathy, a marriage will be destined for either misery or termination. Simply put, those who choose to abandon their marriages due to surmountable conflicts are likely focusing too much on their spouses and not nearly enough on themselves; this again is hypocrisy.

What About Adultery?

In the conservative Christian community, divorce is typically frowned upon as a violation of the Bible's teachings regarding the perpetual union of marriage. This is especially the case regarding divorces for what are deemed to be shallow, emotional reasons. However, it is commonly believed that adultery, regarded as the worst possible violation of the marital covenant, is grounds for a permanent separation. Even people outside the Christian community would agree with this. Thus, it is necessary to address the topic of divorce related to adultery from both Christian and non-Christian perspectives.

Christian Considerations

Several years ago, a prominent leader of a Christian ministry announced that she was divorcing her husband after 29 years of marriage. A few years before, the couple almost divorced over the husband's reported infidelity. However, they were able to work on their relationship, renew their vows, and eventually work towards rebuilding trust and intimacy. Unfortunately, it did not last. Part of the reason given for the separation was described as patterns of behavior on the part of her husband that dishonor God. In other words, the renewed vows were somehow broken again.

My heart goes out to this couple, as well as the many people who may have been impacted by their separation. Divorce is seldom an easy option, and the effects of it can last for years to come. However, the concern in this situation is not only social and emotional, but also theological.

In her Facebook post, this leader explained that she had "clear biblical justification" for pursuing a divorce. After years of trying to salvage her marriage, she affirmed her belief that the Bible supports her heart-wrenching decision. Does it really?

I recognize that this is a very sensitive topic, for the devastation of divorce is both evident and persistent. That said, one assumption that seems to be taken for granted is that the Bible provides "clear . . . justification" for ending one's marriage in certain situations. While she did not admit that infidelity was a primary reason for the divorce, some form of it is implied. Thus, this section will explore the question of whether marital infidelity establishes "clear biblical justification" for divorce.

Before proceeding, I want to clarify that my purpose is not to address whether this leader could have legitimately ended her marriage. I do not have enough details about her situation to address that; nor do I desire them. Rather, the larger question in focus here is whether there is ever "clear biblical justification" for divorce. My argument is that biblical justification for divorce is not nearly as "clear" as many are inclined to believe.

A Biblical Discussion

One of the most prevalent teachings in the evangelical church today is that a Christian has the right to divorce his/her spouse if the other spouse commits adultery. Adultery is understood as engaging in sexual intercourse with another person while married. This teaching is based on the following passage:

> Some Pharisees came to [Jesus] to test him. They asked, "Is it lawful for a man to divorce his wife for any and every reason?" "Haven't you read," he replied, "that at the beginning the Creator 'made them male and female,' and said, 'For this reason a man will leave his father and mother and be united to his wife, and the two will become one flesh.' So they are no longer two, but one flesh. Therefore what God has joined together, let no one separate." "Why then," they asked, "did Moses command that a man give his wife a certificate of divorce and send her away?" Jesus replied, "Moses permitted you to divorce your wives because your hearts were hard. But it was not this way from the beginning. I tell you that anyone who divorces his wife, except for sexual immorality, and marries another woman commits adultery." (Matt. 19:3–9, NIV)

Here, Jesus was responding to the Pharisees' questions concerning the grounds for divorce as they were understood within the Old Testament. But instead of merely answering their questions, he added a new teaching like the pattern seen in his Sermon on the Mount. (Matt. 5–7) There, he highlighted what the Hebrew Scriptures said or how they were interpreted, then provided a new understanding of those teachings with words like "You have heard that it was said. . .But I say unto you. . ." This passage in Matthew 19 is no different; Jesus communicated an Old Covenant understanding while instituting a New Covenant practice for his followers.

In this case, the issue pertains to when a husband can legitimately pursue a divorce from his wife.[5]

There are at least three views on how the last verse in the aforementioned passage is to be understood. Why such differing views? Everything hinges on what the phrase "sexual immorality" (or fornication) means in the context of marriage. How we understand that phrase will substantiate our answer to the question of when/if a believer can separate from a spouse with immunity.

Before we explore the various interpretations of Jesus's words, it should be noted that the phrase "except for sexual immorality" is in italics in most Bibles. This means that these words were not in the most reliable manuscripts used for that particular Bible translation but were added for clarity. If these words were not originally spoken by Jesus, it would suggest that there were no legitimate reasons for a husband to divorce his wife. In fact, this rendering of the verse makes it more consistent with the parallel passages in the other gospels. (see Mark 10:11; Luke 16:18) Nevertheless, for our purposes, we will discuss the passage in depth since it has been the basis upon which many 'Christian' marriages have been dissolved.

A Matter of Interpretation

The first view, and perhaps the most common, holds that the phrase "sexual immorality" refers to adultery. This understanding allows for a justified separation if one's spouse is unfaithful during the marriage. Advocates of this view highlight several observations in support of this interpretation. First, it seems to make sense. After all, the warnings against committing adultery are numerous. (Exod. 20:14; Lev. 20:10; Heb. 13:4) Since adultery is regarded as the worst form of "sexual immorality" in marriage, proponents of this view affirm that the phrase "sexual immorality" as used by Jesus must be a reference to adultery. Furthermore, sex is reserved for marriage only, which is why premarital sex is to be circumvented via marriage. (1 Cor. 7:8–9)

5. There are no biblical teachings or examples allowing wives to divorce their husbands, which explains why this passage is worded as such.

Despite the popularity of this view, there are several reasons to conclude that "sexual immorality" is not a reference to the act of adultery. First, the Greek word from which this phrase is derived is *porneia*, which is usually translated as fornication (i.e. sexual intercourse before marriage, including harlotry or whoredom). The Greek word for adultery is *moicheia*, which is understood as post-marital unfaithfulness. If Jesus was saying that adultery is grounds for divorce, Matthew could have used *moicheia* instead of *porneia*. While this does not mean that adultery is not a form of "sexual immorality" (it certainly is), textually speaking, it appears that Jesus had something else in mind.

Moreover, this understanding does not take into account the other teachings on sin and marriage in the New Testament. For instance, Jesus taught that if someone sins against us (in this case, commits adultery), and later expresses a desire for forgiveness, Christians must forgive him (Matt. 18:21–35). Adultery is not an unforgivable sin, and unforgiveness is never an option for follow-ers of Christ. So, even if the act of adultery gave the Christian the right to end their marriage, they would not be justified in doing so if there was a desire for forgiveness on the part of the offending partner. Surely, we cannot truly forgive a repentant spouse while simultaneously punishing them permanently for their sin. If that was the case, God could fully forgive his people and still send them to hell.

This leads to the second teaching that is related to this topic.

According to the apostle Paul, a Christian spouse who is married to a non-believer (or a believer by extension) is forbidden from divorcing her spouse if the other party wants to remain in the relationship. (1 Cor. 7:12–13) Implied here is that the unbelieving spouse does not want to separate from the Christian spouse and thus wants to continue in the marriage. The prohibition in this passage is clear, making divorce, even if adultery has taken place, unacceptable.

Lastly, in the Old Testament, the Israelites were instructed on how to handle an adulteress wife. (Num. 5:11–31) If she was dis-covered to have been unfaithful, she was to be judged by God, not divorced by her husband. Since the words of Jesus stemmed from the teachings in the Old Testament, they would have been consistent with them. Thus, Jesus would not have suggested that divorce would be allowed in the case of adultery if that would contradict prior teachings on that subject.

Another Understanding?

The second view on what "sexual immorality" constitutes is that it refers to any form of sexual activity that is not within the confines of monogamous marriage. These acts of lust could include practices such as viewing pornography, adultery, intimate touching, bestiality (sexual activity involving animals), etc. Support for this view comes from the fact that the Greek word for "sexual immorality" is not *moicheia* (adultery) but *porneia* (fornication). Accordingly, it is not adultery per se that is in mind, but any behavior that could be considered contrary to God's standards for sexuality within marriage.

Surely, there are several acts of sexual deviance that are condemned in the Old Testament. (i.e. Lev. 18) All the behaviors listed are regarded as sinful, which is why death was the punishment for those who indulged in such practices. If there were multiple types of "sexually immorality" back then, there are multiple actions that could rightfully be grounds for divorce today, the reasoning goes.

Furthermore, Jesus elsewhere said that men could commit adultery in their hearts if they look at women with lustful desire. (Matt. 5:27–28) Thus, a person can be guilty of internal adultery by simply viewing someone lustfully. In that case, with adultery being an example of sexual immorality, viewing others with lustful intentions could also be considered grounds for divorce.

Problems

The first problem with this view is that it interprets the sayings of Jesus in such a way as to extend the reasons for divorcing one's spouse when his emphasis was on limiting them. That is, Jesus appeared to be saying that there is only one exception to the 'no divorce' rule (i.e. sexual immorality), not many exceptions. If Jesus was affirming divorce based on a spouse viewing porn, engaging with animals, or participating in some form of genital stimulation, that would serve to provide multiple reasons to end one's marriage. While none of these practices should be taken lightly, this is precisely the conclusion that Jesus was working against with the Pharisees.

The second problem is that this view is not sufficiently supported by the Scriptures. In both the Old and New Testaments, the prohibitions against sexual deviance are not necessarily discussed in the context of marriage. That is, these general discussions about sexual sin are not connected to any specific marital consequences. Therefore, it is a colossal stretch to apply them to the exception clause within Jesus's teaching on this subject.

Moreover, the parallel passages in other gospels read as follows: "Anyone who divorces his wife and marries another woman commits adultery." (Mark 10:11; Luke 16:18) Accordingly, there is no exception mentioned. Why then does Matthew contain the exception clause? Some commentators suggest that the Matthean inclusion of the "sexual immorality" exception was to legitimize Joseph's attempt to divorce Mary once she was secretly impregnated. At any rate, the way Mark and Luke rendered the verse in question makes it that much more likely that adultery was not considered to provide a basis for marital termination.

Internal Adultery?

In addition, some of these practices are not even alluded to in the Bible, let alone explicitly mentioned. For example, there is nothing in the Bible even remotely similar to the phenomenon of viewing pornography. The acts that are condemned specifically involve physical encounters with another person. That said, what did Jesus mean in his statement about committing adultery in the heart? Is that like watching internet pornography, viewing adult magazines, or even staring at attractive women?

The passage in question reads as follows: "You have heard that it was said, 'You shall not commit adultery.' But I tell you that anyone who looks at a woman lustfully has already committed adultery with her in his heart." (Matt. 5:27–28) As is typical of Jesus's teaching style in the Sermon on the Mount, he went above and beyond the letter of the law to address matters of the heart. In this passage, he was stating that it is not acceptable to simply 'look but don't touch' when one's heart is desirous of the physical encounter. His point seems to be that a man should avoid ogling women (and vice versa) lustfully because his focus is to be exclusively on his wife.

It is not sufficient to merely avoid the physical experience if one's heart truly wants to act on the desire. In that sense, it is his motive (i.e. lust) that is sinful, not merely the act (i.e. looking). Understood in this way, lustful gazes would not establish grounds for divorce as the marriage has not been violated in any definitive way. At best, one could argue that lusting after another person is perhaps evidence of either a sexual addiction or marital dissatisfaction (perhaps due to sexual deprivation, 1 Cor. 7:3–5), but certainly not grounds to end the marriage. Whatever the reason, it is corrigible behavior that couples can work through together.

The final problem with this view was presented before, namely, that it disregards other teachings that should apply to this topic. Both forgiveness and remaining with a struggling spouse are expected of followers of Christ, and for good reasons. When believers sin against God, there is usually a desire for, and a seeking of his forgiveness based upon his love and mercy. There is also the recognition that he commands his children to forgive others both indiscriminately and without limitation. (Luke 17:3–4; Matt. 6:14–15)

Furthermore, when the offended spouse continues with the offending spouse, this reflects God's commitment to never leave or forsake his children. (Heb. 13:5) Interestingly enough, the Lord once spoke about divorcing the Israelites over their spiritual 'adulteries', while simultaneously pleading with them to repent of their sins and be restored. (Jer. 3) Not surprisingly, amidst the sins of his people, God later brought judgment on them while also remaining committed to them. (Jer. 5:7–18)

Final View

The third view on Jesus's statement in Matthew is that "sexual immorality" is a reference to premarital sex that was forbidden in the Old Testament. That is, Jesus was teaching that a man who discovered that his betrothed wife was not a virgin could divorce her due to her unchastity. This view has several lines of support.

First, being a virgin until marriage was expected among women in the Old Testament. (Deut. 22:13–21) Also, priests were only allowed to marry virgins, (Lev. 21:13–15) and the apostle Paul equated virginity to being unmarried since sex was only to occur within marriage. (1 Cor. 7:34) In fact, this expectation was so serious that a man who raped (or seduced) a virgin was required to marry her. (Deut. 22:28–29)[6] Why would a rapist (seducer) be required to marry his victim? Despite how psychologically challenging this might appear to be for the woman, this command was a deterrent to fornication, not a minimizing of it.

The reason the rapist (or seducer) had to marry his victim was because he essentially stole her capacity for marriage since she was no longer a virgin and thus not suitable for marriage. In effect, this command was based on compassion for the woman. If the perpetrator did not marry her, no one could. As such, she would be destined to a lifetime of celibacy while being cared for by her parents. To prevent this, a law was established to keep virgins from being raped (seduced). If it happened, the law ensured that they would still be united in marriage, perhaps bear children, and be provided for throughout their lives.

Returning to the New Testament, this is why Joseph was ready to divorce Mary when he found out she was pregnant.

6. Some interpret this passage as suggesting seduction, not rape. See Paul Copan's *Is God a Moral Monster?*

Although they did not yet officially consummate their marriage, he was still regarded as her "husband" and was prepared to "divorce" her. (Matt. 1:19) Why? As was seen in the Old Testament, Mary was supposed to be a virgin during her betrothal (i.e. legal status beyond engagement but prior to official consummation) as well as on her wedding day. Apparently, being pregnant suggested to Joseph that she was not sexually abstinent. Thus, divorcing her over her fornication would have been consistent with Old Testament teachings.

Problem? Not Exactly

Despite the historical context for this view, it has one criticism, namely, that it could be seen as establishing the first view. That is, cheating on one's spouse during the marriage constitutes grounds for divorce. After all, Mary was in some sense Joseph's wife during the betrothal period. Therefore, this could be viewed as a wife supposedly getting pregnant by someone other than her husband. If regarded in that way, this view is like the first.

The problem with this criticism, however, was cited previously. The word used for "sexual immorality" is a term applying to a deviation prior to marriage, not after it. This is precisely why Paul encouraged single Christians to get married, namely, to avoid premarital sex, or "sexual immorality." (1 Cor. 7:1–2) Again, if adultery is what qualified one for divorce, Jesus would have used the word for adultery. Yes, Joseph and Mary were "married" in a ritualistic sense, but we know that the marriage was not actually consummated until after the betrothal period.

The difference between this view and the others is that here the offense occurs prior to the official marriage, whereas the others address what happens afterwards. Also, there is an Old Testament precedent for a husband divorcing his wife over her premarital promiscuity. However, there is no biblical precedent for ending one's marriage over a post-marital act of infidelity. Furthermore, this view best explains how a term pertaining to sex before marriage can be applied to a married couple. Indeed, the miraculous situation involving Joseph and Mary is consistent with this reality. Yet, neither the first nor the second interpretations of the Matthean passage accomplish this.

New Insights

Even if this view is correct, it is essentially null and void under the New Covenant. The reason being is that there is no New Testament doctrine stating that women should be virgins prior to getting married. Through the atonement of Christ, all sins are forgiven through repentance and faith. While maintaining virginity until marriage is certainly advisable for both men and women, it is not currently a prerequisite for holy matrimony. Thus, understanding "sexual immorality" as premarital promiscuity renders New Testament application on this subject obsolete.

Considering these insights, what can be concluded from this ambiguous topic? First, it is unclear exactly what Jesus had in mind when he used the term that has been translated as "sexual immorality." The most probable suggestion is that it was a reference to an Old Testament practice (i.e. divorcing a pre-marital, promiscuous wife) that the Pharisees would have been aware of. Second, even if adultery is what Jesus was describing, the marriage does not have to end in divorce. From God's perspective, no sin replaces forgiveness, grace, mercy, and commitment. Indeed, God struggled through the spiritual adultery of his people for many centuries, and yet never gave up on them when they repented over their sins. (Hos. 3:1) Likewise, followers of Christ are called to be imitators of God as his dear children. (Eph. 5:1)

The late theologian, pastor, and professor R. C. Sproul summarized the regrettable outcomes associated with the rampant occurrences of divorce in modern times:

> Civil courts are disrupting the commandments of God in granting illicit divorces . . . the institutional church has sanctioned divorce on grounds that are in clear opposition to the teachings of Christ . . . clergymen and counselors throughout the land are recommending

divorce where Christ has prohibited it . . . not only is the sanctity of marriage corrupted by state and church, but also the authority of Christ is flagrantly disobeyed in both spheres over which he is king.[7]

Non-Christian Considerations

How can you view divorce on the grounds of adultery if you are not a Christian? The teachings of the New Testament can apply to your situation as well. Forgiveness, grace, and understanding are not uniquely Christian concepts. As one therapist acknowledges these insights,

> If you're the harmed party, consider couples counseling before filing for divorce on the one hand, or pushing yourself to forgive on the other. Give your unfaithful partner the chance to make reparations and earn back your trust. Give yourself and your relationship the opportunity to heal and grow stronger.[8]

Truly, adultery can be one of the most difficult marital violations to forgive, but it is possible. In fact, I had the privilege of working with a non-Christian couple for several months through this difficult topic. And yet, one of the highlights of my counseling career has been to see them work through their challenges and become a better, stronger couple than they were before. Again, it is possible.

From a clinical perspective, some counselors would suggest that it is better for some couples to uncouple. With mental health considerations in mind, the reasoning is that one's mental and emotional well-being are most important to the individual. Thus, in situations where one or both spouses are failing to mature and work towards marital progress (in addition to committing adultery), separation becomes justified. However, this is not the ideal

7. Sproul, *The Intimate Marriage*, 98–99.
8. Lerner, *Marriage Rules*, 147.

approach, but it could be viewed as a realistic option based on the seriousness of the circumstances.

In most cases, divorce is not the answer; maturity is. In an ideal arrangement, both spouses will pursue personal growth and emotional healing if needed. If they do, it is highly unlikely that either of them will ever decide to end their marriage. Why would they? A growing partner's dream is to be connected to someone who also wants the best for him/herself. Ultimately, when two people find that same quality in each other, they become invincible to the challenges facing couples today.

Helpful Tips

If your marriage is not there yet, hang on; there is hope. The progress that can be made will require both parties' involvement, and that is not too much to ask. After all, you both committed yourselves to the marriage, at least verbally. If you feel alone in your efforts to salvage the relationship, stay encouraged. Time will tell, and experiences will reveal how things will work out.

I close with a word of empathy for those who have experienced the devastation of infidelity. The discussion in this chapter is not meant to minimize the pain of unfaithfulness. No doubt, adultery is one of the worst acts of betrayal that a spouse can experience. However, healing and restoration can occur when two people who love each other are willing to work on the challenges that contributed to the affair. With the help of a competent, professional counselor, any adulterous marriage is within the scope of redemption.

John and Julie Gottman have worked with couples for several decades, witnessing the traumatic effects of marital unfaithfulness time and time again. Yet, they also know how the process of rebuilding trust can happen for those who are committed to it. In the spirit of sensitivity, they explain that when adultery happens,

"Marriage #1 may be gone, but Marriage #2 can be built with a stronger foundation of trust."[9]

Whether adultery occurs in a marriage or not, statistics show that women initiate most divorces in America. One reason for this is because of "lower levels of relationship quality."[10] In light of this, many men believe that the key to having a pleasant marital experience and preventing divorce lies in keeping their wives happy. If husbands can learn how to keep a smile on their wives' faces, all will be well, according to the conventional wisdom of the day. It sounds good, but is it doable? Realistic? Proper? Continue into the next chapter to find out.

Discussion Questions

1. Why do you think many people end their marriages after making permanent vows to their spouses?

2. Is it easy or difficult for you to forgive personal offences? Why?

3. Do you think adultery is a legitimate reason to pursue a divorce? Why or why not?

4. Would you ever advise a friend who is in a difficult marriage to get a divorce? Why or why not?

9. Gottman and Gottman, *10 Principles*, 190.

10. https://www.asanet.org/women-more-likely-men-initiate-divorces-not-non-marital-breakups/ (accessed on 12/10/24)

6

Healthy Wife, Healthy Life

THE COMMON PHRASE 'HAPPY Wife, Happy Life' has made its way into mainstream American life, and many husbands embrace it. Understandably, it seems both reasonable and natural to seek the happiness of one's wife. After all, everyone wants to be happy, and there is little joy in living with an unhappy partner. Thus, this trite cliche has remained a go-to solution for reducing or preventing marital strife, and for some couples, it may be serving them well.

Some men might suggest that pursuing the happiness of their wives is vital to the health of their relationships. Surely, if her happiness is not taken seriously, there may be palpable repercussions. Similarly, if the husband was unhappy, he would want his wife to be attentive and responsive to his feelings. Thus, how can anyone have a problem with the 'happy wife, happy life' approach?

In reality, everything that glitters is not gold, just as everything that is practiced should not be prescribed. These truths are certainly applicable to the topic at hand.

Difficulty with Happiness?

There are several concerns with the notion that focusing exclusively on keeping one's wife happy leads to a happy life. First, it disregards the necessary happiness of the husband for the relationship to be a healthy balance. By placing all the emphasis on the wife's feelings, it puts her at the center of the relationship, when she is not. Both the husband and wife are to be considered when seeking to establish a happy home for one's family.

Moreover, even if the wife is experiencing happiness, the husband might not be. As such, the relationship is likely going to suffer unless his feelings are equally prioritized. As Harriet Lerner aptly explains, "What matters is that two people are dedicated to contributing to each other's happiness."[1]

The second issue with the 'happy wife, happy life' mantra is how insulting it is to the emotional capacity of the wife. The underlying message of this slogan is that a wife who is unhappy is going to make life for her husband (and possibly others) unhappy until her happiness is prioritized. This is clear from the implication that an unhappy wife will lead to an unhappy life. This could represent the height of vengeful immaturity. Like the phrase "hurt people hurt people", such underdeveloped behavior should not be normalized. Indeed, unhappiness is not a license for blatant, spousal mistreatment.

When someone is unhappy or hurting, the unacceptable response is to contribute to someone else's unhappiness or pain. In fact, someone who modeled this in an exemplary fashion was the apostle Paul. After recounting his numerous experiences with suffering, loss, and deprivation, he still managed to focus on the well-being of others. (2 Cor. 11:24–28) There is no indication that his unhappiness was a threat to the happiness of others. To the contrary, he demonstrated how one can receive even brutal, undeserved treatment from others and yet be at peace with the circumstances. Spouses would do well to follow his example of emotional maturity.

Learning to manage one's emotions more effectively should be everyone's pursuit; unfortunately, it is not. Settling for such convenient traps as the 'happy wife, happy life' insult communicates that one's wife does not have the maturity to handle her unhappiness

---

1. Lerner, *Marriage Rules*, 43.

in a more constructive manner. So, in replacing the phrase 'happy wife, happy life' with 'healthy wife, healthy life', this reflects the best marital advice I ever heard, which was "keep growing!"

As couples mature and grow together, happiness can become the natural by-product and not the determining factor in the direction of their relationships.

Happiness Revisited

Another concern with promoting the 'happy wife, happy life' agenda is that happiness is hard to define. Is happiness limited to whatever makes her smile? Of course, smiling, having joy, and other expressions of cheerfulness can be indicators of positive mental health. However, happiness seems to be an elusive and fleeting reality; here today, gone tomorrow.

Over time, the average husband may become more aware of what brings his wife joy, and rightfully so. His efforts may serve him well in those moments of reflection, but they might only be short lived. This is because "Happiness is determined more by one's state of mind than by external events."[2]

Researchers have concluded that marital happiness is oftentimes a reflection of one's premarital happiness. That is, a generally happy bachelor is likely going to be a generally happy husband; the same applies to women.[3] The opposite is also true; those who did not feel good about their lives prior to marriage are more likely to be unhappy upon getting married. The reason is that many times marriage adds very little to one's sense of purpose and personality, which is where one's happiness originates.

Wives who need to be kept happy for the relationship to be enjoyable and stable were probably unhappy in their single state. As such, the reasons for that unhappiness could be more deeply explored to discover any potential trauma from which she may

2. Dalai Lama and Cutler, *The Art of Happiness*, 10.
3. See Parker-Pope, *For Better*.

need healing. Truly, persistent unhappiness can be an indicator of unresolved trauma that is unrelated to the marriage.

In the real world, there are so many things pulling at us daily: work, relationships, children, household responsibilities, spiritual obligations, self-care routines, hobbies, etc. Is it realistic to think that one person has the capacity to keep another person happy amidst all of this? I don't think so. This is yet another reason why this marital approach is so potentially damaging. Overemphasizing happiness for the wife puts an undue burden on the husband to consistently perform up to par in a world that works against our happiness daily. The truth is our happiness is not supposed to be so connected to and derived from another person that we are essentially dependent on them for it.

I remember hearing a woman express how the guy she was dating had only one goal: to make her happy. As we discussed their relationship, I shared how both sweet and shallow it sounded, to which she surprisingly agreed. It sounds lovely, but it is based on naivete. On another occasion, a former co-worker, married for many years, suggested that we develop a lesson on how to keep our wives happy. Although I smiled it off, I knew that I could not in good conscious conduct such a presentation. This 'happy wife, happy life' mindset is pervasive, but also subtly and sincerely misguided.

Happiness Elsewhere?

We sometimes see this happiness trend with first-time mothers. Some of them seem to have their entire identity wrapped up in their exciting new status as a mom. They appear to derive so much joy out of being a parent that it seems as though they become parasitic on their child. Perhaps she has forgotten that the child is there to be raised into responsible adulthood, not to give her life meaning, fulfillment, and of course, happiness. Yes, children can be a blessing to a family, but parents would do well to avoid making idols out of them. This is especially relevant since an unnecessary overemphasis on the child can easily lead to marital distance. For, the mature wife prioritizes her husband over her children; the immature wife prioritizes her children over her husband. Read that last sentence again.

A variety of sources is supposed to enhance our capacity to thrive in the world, regardless of how happy our partner makes us feel. It is simply too great an expectation to put on one person to keep another person happy, especially in a world characterized by stress, division, death, and suffering. Some marital therapists and researchers agree on this point, "Too often, partners can expect or depend on each other to meet every need. This expectation is unrealistic and too great a responsibility for any one partner to bear."[4]

Couples should work together to create an atmosphere of love, sacrifice, and respect between them so that they can naturally contribute to each other's emotional well-being. A one-sided approach will never work in a two-sided marriage.

Lastly, focusing primarily on happiness disregards the potential growth that a wife may need to experience for the couple to have a better marriage. For instance, suppose you agreed to visit a friend's home, who is newlywed, on a bi-monthly basis. Every time you visit, his wife seems to be recovering from a crying spell. Notwithstanding, the couple never says anything about it. Eventually, you decide to ask your friend, out of concern, if everything is okay. Before he responds, it is possible that you have already drawn some negative conclusions about their relationship.

Perhaps he is mistreating her; maybe she feels unloved; they are having a really difficult time adjusting to their first year of marriage. Whatever assumptions you might bring to the discussion, here is one you might not have considered: maybe she is experiencing the growing pains of marriage on the journey towards more relationship maturity. If we are going to jump to conclusions

---

4. Cade et al, "Behavioral and Cognitive Behavioral Therapy with Couples and Families", in Flamez and Hicks, eds., *Marriage, Couple, and Family Therapy*, 357.

about someone's relationship, let's be sure to reflect on the importance of the maturation process prior to taking that leap.

Conclusions

Marital strife accomplishes only what we allow it to. Regarding the scenario, a crying wife does not necessarily indicate any mistreatment on the part of the husband. It could be that she is experiencing challenges that she was not emotionally prepared for. Similarly, the husband could also be dealing with a range of challenging emotions; he may just be better at concealing them. Whatever a couple experiences, sometimes growth and maturity must take precedence over happiness. In fact, if a husband prioritizes his wife's happiness at all costs, even above maturity, he is likely doing his wife a great disservice.

I titled this chapter with a focus on healthy wives because many of them come into marriage in unhealthy mental states. Trauma is not the culprit; refusing to heal is. Truly, healing is a choice, and making a commitment to heal is one of the most important decisions a person will ever make. Simply put, mentally healthy wives make better spouses; mentally unhealthy wives will likely put a significant strain on the marriage. The same is true for husbands.

This is another reason why happiness should not be priority number one; maturity should be. Without healing, there is continued immaturity. Without maturity, there is no growth. When growth is lacking, the result is low-quality, insipid, stressful marriages. Our society does not need any more of these.

I will share more about the book of Proverbs in the next chapter, but for now, here is a passage that is relevant to this topic:

> A wife of noble character is her husband's crown, but a disgraceful wife is like decay in his bones. (Prov. 12:4)

The way towards developing noble character is healing, maturity, and growth. Your marriage should be deemed worthy of these pursuits. If it is, the only question left to answer is, "How do we develop the maturity needed for a healthy marriage?" Answers to that question are only a chapter away.

Discussion Questions

1. What are your thoughts on the phrase, "Happy wife, happy life"?

2. It has been said that mothers typically receive more parenting credit than fathers. Do you think this is also true about wives and husbands? Why or why not?

3. How much should we rely on others for our happiness?

7

Developing Marital Maturity

As you approach the end of the book, it seems necessary to include a discussion on strategies that can cultivate a maturing lifestyle. Each of these practices can be helpful to those who sincerely want better for themselves and their marriages. Ultimately, how important relationship maturity is to you will be reflected in the approach you take regarding these steps towards personal growth.

#1: Be honest with yourself.

Is there trauma from your past that you have never healed from? Are the effects of that neglect sabotaging your marriage? If so, are you open to meeting with a counseling professional who can help you along the healing process? If your answers to these questions are yes, you have reached a level of authenticity that is worthy of celebration. Congratulations, you are on the right track. However, if your answers are no, but they should be yes, you are not being honest with yourself.

Trauma that goes unresolved has negative effects on our lives, emotionally, physically, and mentally. This is the reason that many marriages do not survive. Usually, we think that a divorce results from something tragic that happened during the marriage.

However, we should at least consider what happened before the marriage that should have been confronted but wasn't. Remember this, healing is not a luxury to avoid, it is a treasure to pursue. Only those who discover this truth realize its undeniable value.

After reflecting on her own marriages, Jennifer White shared these insights and considerations with new brides,

> Marriage has a way of causing unresolved emotional issues to float to the surface . . . Are your reactions revealing that you brought a wounded heart to your marriage . . . There is hope, and I'm living proof of that.[1]

The truth is unresolved trauma is responsible for many marital dissolutions. Why? When healing does not follow trauma, immaturity persists, along with mental stagnation. If only couples had been honest enough to confront their unhealthy emotional states, perhaps their marriages might have survived the struggles.

Furthermore, unresolved trauma is also the culprit behind much of the unhappiness people experience. Chances are that unhappy spouses were likely unhappy bachelors or bachelorettes who successfully managed to conceal their discontents. Well, the time is over for deceitful concealment; it is time for honest acknowledgment.

Renee Grace articulated this understanding very poignantly in her recent article entitled "Why We Can't Get Relationships Right,"

> When we recognize that our triggers, insecurities, and unmet emotional needs often stem from past experiences, we can take responsibility for our healing instead of unconsciously projecting these struggles onto our partners. By doing the inner work, we create space for relationships to thrive—where mutual understanding, compassion, and growth can flourish.[2]

---

1. White, *Prayers for New Brides*, 211–12.
2. Grace, *Brainz Magazine*.

Being Humble

Humility is the quality of seeing ourselves for who we truly are, baggage included. Indeed, one can have self-esteem while being humble simultaneously; in fact, we should have both traits. Maintaining self-esteem helps us feel empowered and equipped to face any of the challenges we encounter. Being humble keeps us grounded in reality, and also helps us avoid the traps of arrogance and self-sufficiency.

For those of us already married, we cannot change who we were on our wedding days, but we can change who we become afterwards. If you really want better for both you and your marriage, it begins with honesty. Only then can we discover the benefits of introspection and the necessity of growth. Harriet Lerner agrees, "The best way to work on a relationship always includes working on yourself."[3]

One way to work on ourselves is to increase both the quantity and quality of our protective factors. These are present realities that strengthen our mental well-being while enhancing our resilience in the face of challenges.[4] As a counselor, I have utilized these factors in my sessions with clients, and they have contributed to healthy discussions and positive results. Examples of protective factors include:

- Social support (having people to talk to and get help from when needed)
- Sense of purpose (feeling meaningfully involved in one's roles)
- Coping skills (demonstrating awareness and management of emotions)
- Physical health (embracing a healthy diet and regular exercise)

3. Lerner, *Marriage Rules,* 89.

4. https://www.therapistaid.com/therapy-worksheet/protective-factors (accessed on 2/7/25)

- Healthy thinking (combatting ruminations with rationality)
- Self-esteem (valuing one's self and one's abilities)

Whatever your marital situation, increasing your protective factors can yield positive results in virtually every area of your life, including your relationship.

The pursuit of maturity is ongoing; as more of our subconscious ways are revealed to us, opportunities to grow will be ever-present. When this approach is taken seriously, developing more maturity will become like second nature. As we pursue honesty within ourselves, maturity can become the norm, and our spouses will be the recipients of our progress. Hopefully, we will be the recipient of theirs as well.

#2: Commit to learning from the past.

The saying that those who fail to learn from the past are doomed to repeat it makes sense. When a lesson is not learned (not internalized), it does not have the impact it otherwise would. For example, if a child does not learn to respect her parents, she will continue disrespecting them. If an employee fails to grasp the necessity of punctuality, he will eventually get fired. Similarly, if a husband does not learn how to best demonstrate love and care for his wife, she may continue to view him with resentment. If his wife fails to learn how to value and respect him, she will likely be viewed with disdain.

Behaviors are reinforced based on the consequences or lack thereof. If we commit to learning from the past, we can become more intentional about how we live in the present, as well as prepare for the future.

In marriage, couples tend to make decisions that bring with them crucial learning opportunities. However, not everyone sees them that way. For some, problematic decisions are simply gateways to arguments and strife. Yet, if we reframe these disappointing times as chances to discover how to do things better in the future, they will be much more meaningful in the long run.

When we prioritize marriage, we show through our actions that we are genuinely thoughtful about it. We recognize that callousness, disregard, and vengefulness have no place in such a sacred relationship. As such, committing to learn how to conduct ourselves better than we did in the past is one of the most rewarding ways to honor our promises to our spouses. Failure to do so will likely contribute to repeating cycles of discontent, disillusionment, and even regrets about being in the relationship.

A couple of examples may be helpful. If we have a tendency towards passive listening, we can learn how to become more active and present when our partners are speaking. If we have a bad habit of interrupting our spouses when they are speaking, we can discipline ourselves by developing a considerate level of patience. If we have not been taking our spouses' concerns seriously, we can decide today that we will give careful attention to anything that bothers them. As we apply conscious, consistent effort to doing better in these and other areas, relationship stressors can become the exception rather than the norm.

#3: Apply the book of Proverbs to your life.

The biblical book of Proverbs, located within the Old Testament (Hebrew Bible), is among history's most influential literary sources. Why? The primary focus of the book is attaining wisdom, oftentimes contrasting the ways of the wise with those of fools. Here is one example:

> Do not rebuke mockers or they will hate you; rebuke the
> wise and they will love you. (Prov. 9:8)

There are two categories of responders in this verse: wise and mockers (i.e. fools). Their responses to being rebuked are based on who they are, not what is communicated. According to dictionary. com, rebuke is defined as "to express sharp, stern disapproval of; reprove; reprimand." Why do the two categories of people have different responses if they both have presumably done something worthy of criticism? Wise (mature) people are receptive to growth;

mockers (immature) are not. That is, the wise person can receive and appreciate unpleasant criticisms, while the foolish person cannot and thus dismisses them.

As you reflect on this passage, ask yourself, "How do I respond to constructive criticism? Do I see it as a trigger to become defensive or an opportunity for growth?" Remember, anyone can tell us what we want to hear; not everyone will tell us what we need to hear. Maturity demands that we value those who love us enough to tell us the truth about ourselves.

Here is another example:

> A wise son brings joy to his father, but a foolish son brings grief to his mother. (Prov. 10:1)

Although this proverb relates to the parent-child relationship, it could be applied to others as well. The message seems to be that wise (mature) children bring joy to their parents, while foolish (immature) children bring sadness. The implication is that the children in question are of reasonable age to make either wise or foolish decisions. If we extend this principle to marital relationships, we could say that the wise (mature) spouse brings joy to their partner, while foolish (immature) spouses bring sadness.

Many other examples could be provided, but you get the point. I encourage you, whatever your thoughts are about the Bible, to read and apply the book of Proverbs to your life (where applicable). You may receive new insights and challenges as you implement the teachings therein and consequently move towards a greater level of both maturity and wisdom.

#4: Fill your life with growth-oriented material.

One of the reasons it is crucial for parents to limit and monitor what their children are exposed to is because of the likelihood of natural internalization. Children absorb things in the world like a sponge, and they have the capacity to retain it for years to come. If they are surrounded by toxicity, drama, and immature parenting, they will inevitably internalize much of that to their detriment.[5] In contrast, if children are consumed with positivity (not the toxic kind), kindness, and mature parenting, they will reap the benefits of that environment.

Adults are similar.

If we are not indulging in the right kinds of materials, it will work against us in subtle ways. If we are, those resources can strengthen our resolve to continue on the path towards passionate self-improvement. What materials am I referring to? Ask yourself the following diagnostic questions:

- Are the things I watch on TV or online contributing to my growth?

- Is what I enjoy listening to (music or otherwise) contributing to my growth?

- Are my attitudes and perspectives on life contributing to my growth?

- Are the places I visit for personal reasons contributing to my growth?

- Are the things I read contributing to my growth?

- Are the people I am closely associated with contributing to my growth?

More on people.

Regardless of our social status, the influence of others in our lives may be undeniable. We may not always recognize it, but it is there. The issue is not whether others influence us, but how we allow ourselves to be influenced. Ideally, those closest to us would serve as positive associations, but this is not always the case.

Since I have already expressed my value for the book of Proverbs, I am taking the liberty to share another verse here:

> Walk with the wise and become wise, for a companion of fools suffers harm. (Prov. 13:20)

---

5. See Gibson, *Adult Children of Emotionally Immature Parents.*

Again, we see the contrast between who the wise (mature) person should align himself with; those characterized by wisdom, not those known for their folly. Friendships are certainly meaningful if they amount to mutual investments, but not if they entail toxic influencers that reinforce immaturity. Perhaps this is why the proverb warns against keeping company with the wrong kinds of people; if they are not leading you up higher, chances are they may end up bringing you lower.

The Challenge

Now that you have encountered several diagnostic questions related to growth, what changes do you need to make? It is not enough to merely acknowledge our growth detractors while taking no corrective actions to remove them. Surely, growth requires sacrifice. Are any sacrifices needed for you to move forward in your life and marriage? Remember, be honest.

How does this relate to marital obligations? The spouses we become result from our daily routines. If virtually none of our habits reflect a desire for growth, that will likely show up in the marriage in adverse ways. Likewise, if there are numerous practices we engage in that are cultivating growth in our lives, that can certainly enhance the relationship.

For example, consider the marriage where one spouse is consumed with watching soap operas, crime shows, and reality dramas. The other spouse enjoys watching documentaries, current events, and shows with educational content. They never watch TV together due to the differences in taste. As a result, they will be disconnected in this area of their relationship. Consequently, they will miss out on opportunities for stimulating conversations related to their viewing choices. In this case, it seems that the latter spouse may be more focused on learning/growth than the former. Now, imagine how much better their marriage could be if they were more mutually aligned in their orientation towards growth.

Another example is when one partner has a consistent workout routine while the other almost never exercises on a regular basis. The first spouse is prioritizing their physical health far more than the second one. If things remain the same, that could lead to resentment on the part of the more health-conscious partner. Surely, lifestyle-related illnesses are as common as sunrises. Yet, this awareness still does not lead some spouses to take better care of themselves. Again, imagine the bond that could be created if both spouses took their physical health more seriously.

As I stated previously, one of the best things we can do for both us and our spouses is "keep growing." Every day presents opportunities to better ourselves; all we have to do is identify and respond to them. Hopefully, you see your marriage as worth the effort.

To summarize, things we can do to pursue marital maturity include:

1. Being honest with ourselves about the potential need for healing from trauma (including the need for counseling);

2. Committing to learning from our past decisions/reactions in order to do better with them in both the present and the future;

3. Applying the book of Proverbs to our lives to reap the benefits of a life characterized by wisdom; and

4. Filling our lives with growth-oriented materials that are investments in our journey towards increasing maturity.

By now, I trust you have a better understanding of how healing (or the lack thereof), trauma, maturity/immaturity, and growth (or stagnation) impact marriages. But before you shelve this book, I must revisit my earlier discussion by sharing a few concluding remarks.

Discussion Questions

1. How challenging is it for you to revisit your past in consideration of the possible need for present healing?

2. Describe something you have learned about your thoughts, words, or behaviors that has helped you do better with them.

3. What are your thoughts on applying the book of Proverbs to your life?

4. Are most of the things you spend your time on helping or hindering you? How?

8

Conclusion

I WROTE THIS BOOK primarily for three categories of people: those who are considering marriage, those already married, and counselors who work with married couples. My comments below are summary points for those within these groups.

Considering Marriage

Marriage can be a beautiful journey, having the love of your life beside you as you navigate the vicissitudes of life. It can also be one of the most disappointing experiences one will ever have. The relationship will become what both you and your partner make of it. Ultimately, the outcome of your marriage depends on the level of maturity you both bring to the table, as well as cultivate throughout your marital experience.

If you proceed with tying the knot, I hope you will embrace the necessity of your continued growth to have a rewarding, sustainable marriage. I also wish the same for your spouse, so that you both can reap the benefits of lifelong, marital satisfaction.

Already Married

You can probably relate to much of what I have shared in earlier chapters. Wherever you are in your relationship, my hope for you is similar to those who have yet to experience holy matrimony. Keep growing, even if your spouse is not. Do it for your own mental health and well-being. If you have neglected the prioritization of maturity in your marriage, but your spouse has not, consider getting on board with him/her. It is never too late to begin growing in new ways.

You owe it to both yourself and your spouse to strive to be a better version of yourself. After all, you made a promise, established a covenant, with your partner. As a teammate in the game of life, players are to work hard so that the team will win. How has your contribution to the team been? Lethargic or impassioned? A resolve to honor our commitments is one of the most noble qualities one can possess. Indeed, spouses honor their commitments to each other by pursuing marital maturity and thereby creating an atmosphere of growth in their lives and their homes. May this be true of your marriage both now and always.

Marriage Counselor

I understand that in counseling, there are certain approaches that are supposed to be taken with clients. Incidentally, some of the things I communicated in this book I would not present in a counseling session. Here, I can be more direct and challenging than I would if I was meeting with a couple. Nevertheless, the points made throughout, with a little tweaking, can facilitate helpful conversations with couples in distress. I hope you agree.

As counselors, we want to help our clients live better, more enriching lives. Yet, we know that sometimes they need to uncover dormant realities that have been either resisted or suppressed. I believe books like this can help us build a stronger therapeutic alliance with clients and thereby assist them in greater ways with accomplishing their goals. As we know, the better prepared counselors are, the more likely it is that clients will have progressive, transformative, therapeutic experiences. Let's continue to grow in our own maturity so that we can help clients do the same.

Whatever your status, thank you for reading *Marriage and Maturity*. Now, please share it with or recommend it to someone else.

Discussion Questions

1. If you are single, have you read anything here that either encouraged or discouraged you regarding a future marriage?

2. If you are married, what was one insight shared that could be beneficial to your marriage?

3. If you are a marriage counselor, can you describe one point from the book that could be helpful to your clients?

Bibliography

American Counseling Association. 2014. *ACA Code of Ethics*. Alexandria, VA.

Cade, Rochelle, Esther Benoit, Katherine Hermann-Turner, and Robika Mylroie. 2019. "Behavioral and Cognitive Behavioral Therapy with Couples and Families." In *Marriage, Couple, and Family Therapy: Theory, Skills, Assessment, and Application,* edited by Brande Flamez, & Janet Hicks, 343-Solana Beach, CA: Cognella.

Copan, Paul. 2011. *Is God a Moral Monster? Making Sense of the Old Testament God.* Grand Rapids, MI: Baker.

Diamond, Jed. 2016. *The Enlightened Marriage: The 5 Transformative Stages of Relationships and Why the Best is Still to Come.* Wayne, NJ: Career.

Direnfeld, Gary. 2013. *Marriage Rescue: Overcoming Ten Deadly Sins in Failing Relationships.* Far Hills, NJ: New Horizon.

Dweck, Carol. 2007. *Mindset: The New Psychology of Success.* New York: Ballantine.

Endrei, Paul and Patti Endrei. 2008. *Glue: Sticking Power for Lifelong Marriages.* Westlake, OH: Insight.

Fillmore, Dana and Amy Barnhart. 2011. *Happily Ever After: How To Be Happily Married to the One You Already Married.* San Diego, CA: Have a Sweet Life.

Fraenkel, Peter. 2011. *Sync Your Relationship, Save Your Marriage: Four Steps to Getting Back on Track.* New York: Palgrave Macmillan.

Gibson, Lindsay. 2015. *Adult Children of Emotionally Immature Parents: How to Heal from Distant, Rejecting, or Self-Involved Parents.* Oakland, CA: New Harbinger.

Gottman, Julie, and John Gottman. 2015. *10 Principles for Doing Effective Couples Therapy.* New York: W. W. Norton and Co.

Grace, Renee. 2024. "Why We Can't Get Relationships Right." *Brainz Magazine,* Dec. 12–19.

Harvey, Dave. 2007. *When Sinners Say "I Do": Discovering the Power of the Gospel for Marriage.* Wapwallopen, PA: Shepherd.

Lerner, Harriet Goldhor. 2012. *Marriage Rules: A Manual for the Married and the Coupled Up.* New York: Avery.

Lewis, C. S. 2001. *Mere Christianity*. San Francisco, CA: HarperOne.

Northrup, Chrisanna, Pepper Schwartz; and James Witte. 2012. *The Normal Bar: The Surprising Secrets of Happy Couples and What They Reveal About Creating a New Normal in Your Relationship*. New York: Harmony.

Parker-Pope, Tara. 2011. *For Better: How the Surprising Science of Happy Couples Can Help Your Marriage Succeed*. New York: Plume.

Roberson, Calvin. 2021. *Marriage Ain't for Punks: A No-Nonsense Guide to Building a Lasting Relationship*. New York: FaithWords.

Runkel, Hal and Jenny Runkel. 2011. *Screamfree Marriage: Calming Down, Growing Up, and Getting Closer*. New York: Crown Archetype.

———. 2012. *The Self-Centered Marriage: The Revolutionary Scream-Free Approach to Rebuilding Your "We" By Reclaiming Your "I"*. New York: Three Rivers.

Sproul, R. C. 2003. *The Intimate Marriage: A Practical Guide to Building a Great Marriage*. Philipsburg, NJ: P & R.

Van Der Kolk, Bessel. 2014. *The Body Keeps the Score: Brain, Mind, and Body in the Healing of Trauma*. New York: Penguin.

White, Jennifer. 2015. *Prayers for New Brides: Putting on God's Armor After the Wedding Dress*. Green Forest, AR: New Leaf.

Xiv, Dalai Lama and Howard Cutler. 2009. *The Art of Happiness: A Handbook for Living*. New York: Riverhead.

About the Author

JASON L. MOORE IS a licensed professional counselor who has worked with children, teens, adults, families, groups, and couples. He has served as Executive Director of a family care center, and is certified in suicide prevention (QPR), mediation (Cleveland Mediation Center), and premarital counseling (SYMBIS). Jason is a member of the Christian Association for Psychological Studies.

In addition, Jason works as an adjunct instructor in philosophy and religious studies at Cuyahoga Community College in Cleveland, Ohio. Previously, he was a visiting instructor in theology at Notre Dame College of Ohio and is currently a Ph.D. candidate in theology at the University of South Africa. Jason is also the author of *Divine Frustrations: Exploring the Most Challenging Complaints About God.*

For more information, visit www.jasonlmoore.com.